SACRED GROUND
&
HOLY WATER

TRAVEL TALES OF ENLIGHTENMENT

SACRED GROUND & HOLY WATER

TRAVEL TALES OF ENLIGHTENMENT

LYN FUCHS

coffeetownpress

Seattle, WA

Coffeetown Press
Seattle, Washington
Published by Coffeetown Press
PO Box 70515
Seattle, WA 98127

Cover design by Sabrina Sun
Contact: info@coffeetownpress.com
Copyright © 2010 by Lyn Fuchs

ISBN: 978-1-60381-087-6 (Paper)
ISBN: 978-1-60381-088-3 (Cloth)
ISBN: 978-1-60381-089-0 (ePub)

Contents

My Deepest Fear

Innocence, in a sense, dies when fear is born.

Vancouver Island doesn't seem like the place to confront terror. Sailing, windsurfing, and kayaking don't seem like ways to do so. Yet it was, and they were. You see, my deepest fear is just that: phobia of the deep. This began with a near drowning, thrashing about wrapped in tentacles—I'll come back to that later.

Saturday, I rode a crisp, isle-bound breeze out of English Bay with my buddy, Rob, his black mutt, Wally, and two bikini-clad friends. (Vanquishing inner demons need not be unpleasant.)

We hoisted the sails. Virgin cloth unfurled in whip-cracking independence before succumbing to Calypso's caress. Wedding-white tufts billowed in a marriage of wind and craft, giving birth to speed.

W.O. Mitchell described prairie as the least common denominator of nature: land and sky; all around me was aqua prairie. I saw the blue, felt the spray, heard the roar, tasted the salt.

Gripping a taut line allowed me to lean out and peer down. Coho Salmon skiffed the surface. A luminous smack of Moon Jellies drifted in the murky depths. I imagined the colossal White Sturgeon and Pacific Octopus skulking far below. I imagined there were things down there I couldn't imagine.

Suddenly, a signature sound spun my head like a Pavlovian bell. Uncapped beer! An ice-sweating bottle was pressed into my sweat-sweating hand. I indulged immoderately. (Breakfast is the most important meal of the day.)

More brews pressed themselves into my hand till a thought struck me: I had never fly cast from a sailboat. No one that I knew had. Why anglers never stand on a rocking deck whizzing a hook back and forth past ropes, sails, and human appendages was beyond me. Fetching my rod, I swaggered off to pioneer the sport… Discovering the ocean lacked fish, I set about untangling my line.

Splash! Rob fell overboard. With an "I-meant-to-do-that" smirk, he beckoned us to swim. Only loyal Wally responded. Once afloat, the panicky pup couldn't reboard. Attempting to board Rob instead, the hapless hound clawed a shirtless swimmer. Rob howled. Orgasmic at this display of canine affinity, Wally howled in harmony. By the time we hauled them aboard, man/beast bonding had shredded Rob bloody.

"You look like a skinned elk!"

"You still look like a $%#!"

While Lori and Angie doted over our wounded sailor, I wondered what injuries I could incur.

Lori went below deck to pee. "Oh, my gosh! Angie! You gotta see these cute, little nautical fixtures." Directly above, Angie opened a hatch and began photographing Lori on the toilet. Rob and I exchanged "pinch-me-I'm-dreamin" glances as adolescent fantasy #47 was fulfilled.

At dusk, we coasted into the shallows of a remote skerry. China Rockfish fled from our approach as Sea Anemones waved us in. Harbor Seals and Steller Sea Lions issued a honking, barking intruder alert.

Calling it a night, we anchored off the rocky islet. Wispy trees clung to bleached boulders like nymphs embracing hulks. Being gentlemen, we let the girls sleep on the boat. Being drunk, we offered to sleep on the girls.

Sunrise and a squawking gull came about five minutes later. Wally's tongue woke all slackers. We cast off quietly, barely rippling the still, glassy waters, and drifted like a ghost ship into the Georgia Strait.

All morning, a lone cloud raced our boat: two parallel ovals crossing azure planes without perceptible motion. An inquisitive Pacific White-sided Dolphin briefly broke the monotony. Finding us boring, he moved on.

Midday sun. Shadows disappeared from the deck; shimmerings appeared on the horizon. Baked-brain euphoria. We docked at Parksville with glowing skin and dangerous bliss. Swapping sea legs for Highway 4 and a Ford Explorer, we started across the island.

Our first stop was Cathedral Grove. This towering stand of cedars goes back over eight hundred years. These trees remember when the Americas were an infinite wilderness: the last worthy staging ground for a man's primal dreams.

For me, old-growth forest is sacred ground. Like F. Scott Fitzgerald, "I held my breath for a transitory enchanted moment in the presence of this continent, compelled into an aesthetic contemplation I neither understood nor desired, face to face for the last time in history with something commensurate to my capacity for wonder."

Abandoning such noble reflections, I attempted to impress the babes by hyperbolizing the California Redwoods, (snow job falling on cedars). Rob would not be outdone. Offering a glimpse of even bigger timber, he reached for his zipper as I hastily changed the subject.

The drive to Nitinat Lake gave me time to panic. Sailing was one thing; windsurfing and kayaking were another. The watery abyss and I were about to get better acquainted. I remembered how fearless I used to be.

One childhood summer, my Dad and I climbed Half Dome. This lightning-charred geological celebrity, with its round back and sheer vertical face, has reined over Yosemite for eons, awaiting the attentions of its personal paparazzi, Ansel Adams. Our trek was a historical footnote, except in the mind of a young boy.

We set up base camp just below the summit ascent. Didn't sleep much. A group of nearby nudists smoked herb and shuffled DNA. I was fascinated, and repulsed. (Getting back to nature may be great, but exposure to the elements had eroded these hippies rather harshly.)

Our boots hit the upward trail at dawn. Trees and clouds in turn deserted us to our sol companion: the relentless sun. After a rest just long enough for chipmunks to spoil our water, we poured the contaminated life-nectar on the ground.

My father was breathing hard. Suddenly, I realized that while I was growing up, he was growing old. "I guess we better turn around," he panted. "If I go much farther, I won't make it back down."

Glaring at him with fire in my eyes, I snapped, "Dad, we never said we'd make it back down; we just said we'd make it to the top!"

Bravado comes easy for kids. Not understanding life's value, they wager the commodity freely. Inhibition comes easy for adults. Not appreciating life's brevity, they let caution steal their dreams. A little fear is good, but it must be mastered.

We finally reached the dreaded loch. Nitinat Lake is an inlet that acts as a sea-breeze-collecting wind tunnel. Picture a hurricane, with a crowded campground.

Rob tossed me a slimy, foul-smelling wetsuit, probably harboring more unseen critters than any body of water. I suited up with all the optimism of a Texas inmate filing for clemency. Grabbing our gear, we trudged to the shore.

In seamless motion, Rob hopped on his board, popped up his sail, and snagged a passing gust. Lori and Angie looked at me for a duplicate performance. I got on, fell off, got on, fell off, etc., etc., etc.

Some time later, I was saddling the wind and riding the range. Yee Haw! Then, it hit me: the longer I stayed up, the farther out I'd go. Every second I surfed was ten feet of algae I'd swim. Oh, the injustice! Rode that little Philly to the middle of the corral. Then, the wind died. "Son-of-a—" Kersploosh!

Sputtering and thinking happy thoughts, I dog-paddled the rig through primordial broth. Rubbery, decomposing vegetation fondled my toes. I couldn't resist a flashback to when this paranoia began.

One childhood Spring, I was tubing down some torrential snowmelt. The brown, interchangeable forestry sign proclaimed the river safe. This satisfied my parents. (The only rafting reassurance I, Huckleberry Lyn, needed would have read: "Objects in icy mountain water are not as small and shriveled as they appear.")

Shooting over white, foamy moguls, I rounded a bend. Instantly, the water became still, deep, and green. Leaves circled aimlessly in whirlpools. Shade cooled the air and shadowed the sandy bottom. Submerged in the emerald calm was a hollow, fallen tree.

I dove down for a closer look. Breaststroking into the cavernous root tangle, my sandal snagged. A first freeing attempt failed. My lungs emptied; my confidence vanished. In a panicked frenzy, I hallucinated that the roots were giant squid tentacles. Instead of unbuckling the tiny leather shackles, I yanked and yanked, losing consciousness.

Lying one-shoed and gasping on the bank, I remembered nothing of my escape to the realm of air. Dad and I searched all afternoon for the sandal. We didn't find it, because I didn't take him to the same place. To plagiarize Norman Maclean, I am haunted by waters. My fears merge into one, and a river runs through it.

So there I was at Nitinat, encircled again by writhing plants. This time I stayed cool. Neptune granted me safe passage; sea dragons took a holiday. I sloshed ashore as Rob readied the kayaks. Forgetting to be scared, I was soon mid-lake, doin' the oar-and-torso boogie.

"Flip over!" Rob commanded. Flip over? Voluntarily? This was certainly counter-intuitive. Rob explained that a safe recovery is your basic kayaking skill. Hmmm. Sounded like a terrorist plot to me. I reached down deep, mustering a force even stronger than fear: male ego—you know, never let 'em see ya sweat, better dead than chicken, that sort of thing.

I flipped over. There is nothing more stimulating than looking at the reflective undersurface of a lake with a deluge surging up your nose. Did I say stimulating? I meant horrifying and nauseating.

Rob left me floundering, just long enough to pay for everything I'd ever done to him—real or imagined. Then he paddled alongside so I could use his kayak to right myself. I practiced over and over till flipping became smooth.

All the way home, I savored my little victory—small step for mankind, big step for me. Nearing Vancouver, we dropped sail. A full moon hung in cobalt over the city's glittering-pearl skyline; snowcapped mountains saw-toothed across the horizon; sultry rhythms floated over from the Jericho Beach Jazz Festival.

While Angie grilled salmon, zucchini, and portabellas, Rob popped a cork. Lori stuffed a morsel of sourdough and Brie into my mouth as I garbled out, "If this is terror, I could probably get used to it."

Thus ends a ritual voyage from boyhood to manhood, from fallacies to phalluses. I no longer fear deep, dark waters. (Now, I fear brewski: lurking in those clear, golden waters are excess carbs and impaired seamanship.) Water was the spawning ground of my fears. Following life's cycle, I returned to the source.

Fear, in a sense, becomes the birthplace of courage.

Wandering Under the Southern Cross

Nobody yelled "Fire!" Instead, frantic cries were snuffed out by the crush of bodies swarming an exit. Smoke and panic spread across the stuffy theatre like a Napoleonic battlefield, while passing stampedes of legs and butts cast monstrous shadows on the movie screen. Then orange, crackling flames began licking over the balcony. Should I sit and fry or jump up and be trampled? My hands claw-gripped the armrests as my feet nervously tap-tap-tapped, crunching spilled popcorn. Had I come halfway around the planet only to die watching a bad Sylvester Stallone flick? My mind drifted back a few months to when this odyssey began.

My journey commenced near Lake Victoria. I swung the machete violently. I panted like an animal. The sticky vines and steamy air playfully argued whether I should be strangled or suffocated. My blade's rhythmic thud feebly voiced my dissent. Trekking through Kenyan rainforest is more like gardening than hiking. Running down my back, red ants and perspiration were indistinguishable. If I swatted it, it was sweat. If I ignored it, it was alive. By noon I'd surrendered my flesh to a wildlife habitat: a playground for all creatures so inclined.

My companions were Kipsigi hunters. They'd never had a friend as pale as elephant tusk; I'd never had a friend as black as tire rubber. We tried not to stare. Such awkwardness didn't diminish our bond. When climbing together, a leathery hand becomes a rope, a grimy shoulder becomes a step, and a tired grin becomes a pact. Instinct runs deep within a species. We six humans instinctively formed a clan against the wilderness.

We intersected a dry streambed. Strolling along its soft, reddish clay was a refreshing change. Above us, the forest canopy was dense. Rain from the week before still dripped leaf to leaf, each crystal droplet choosing its intricate path to the jungle floor. We passed flowers ranging from the sublime to the grotesque, with colors ranging from sunny yellow to bloody purple, aromas from syrupy sweet to hypnotic spice.

Monkeys howled and screeched overhead. Swinging past us, they laughed. "Okay," I shouted, "Maybe our arms are too short for transportation." Glancing at my comrades, I saw the monkeys weren't alone in doubting my competence, so I shut up. Single filing along, our strides melded into a cadence.

Suddenly, the front man stopped. The rest of us bumped in turn, like bad slapstick. Pointing at the ground, he hissed an unknown Swahili word. The others encircled the spot, tossing the word back and forth into a hissing symphony. Kipsigis point with their lips, so the group alternately puckered toward the ground, as if kissing invisible lovers. The hissing and kissing continued for some time. Finally the leader gave me a trembling translation: "Fresh leopard feet! Leopard smell and track man. Leopard no fear fire. We go now!"

We continued toward the soon-expected village. First, at a brisk walk. Then, after a couple UFNs (Unidentified Forest Noises), at a brisk run. We abruptly burst out of the dim forest into the middle of a blazing African day. Our eyes adjusted and blinked at an enchanted scene.

Out of the jungle flowed a river: a serpentine, meandering, chocolate-colored river, clouded with nutrient-rich, botanical sediment. Along the bank, crocodiles napped and hippos grazed. Across the wide valley of golden cornfields was another river: a swift, clear, boisterous river, tumbling out of the emerald green hills. It crossed an enormous slab of exposed, polished rock where it shattered into a thousand miniature waterfalls. Beneath the cascades, veiled by mist and framed by rainbows, was an ancient wooden house and waterwheel. Inside, a rotating stone ground corn into meal—and apparently had done so since the dawn of time.

Where the rivers met was a miracle: the combined waters flowed on neatly divided—half muddy, half clear. Farther along, the spirits of the hills and forest resigned themselves into one. In the "v" of the merging rivers, spotted cattle chewed complacently on a grassy slope. The slope ascended a high bluff, perched above the whole panorama. Here sat a single hut, surrounded by sugarcane and fruit trees. No one spoke to break the spell, but we all simultaneously began the ascent to the obvious destination.

The occupant was a wrinkled little man who walked with a stick. His earlobes, pierced with bulky wooden adornments, had stretched several inches. He raised corn. He had no idea how old he was. We tried to discern his age, using every mathematical system we could remember or invent. We decided he was real old.

We drank tea and talked. Walked to his son's house, drank tea, and talked. Walked to his relative's house, drank tea, and talked. Walked to his friend's house, drank tea, and talked. The impatience of my culture and mega doses of caffeine reached critical mass. I blurted out, "Why do we sit around all day, drink tea, and talk?"

The old man responded innocently, "Can you make the corn grow faster?"

I could have "enlightened" him—after all, my technological civilization produces genetic hybrids that do just that—but it would've distracted from his profound truth: there are forces in life bigger than I. Perhaps that's why I wander: some instinctive spiritual quest. Do I travel to know a higher reality, the world, or just myself? I finished my tea.

A rooster crowed. I opened my eyes to the sight of thatched roof, inches above. The sun filtered through, warming the grass smell from my straw mattress. Bath day! I sprang from bed like a pouncing cheetah, out the door, past the goat, and down a steep hill. Trudging up the road was an old woman. Her gray head balanced the water bucket; her hunched back bore the firewood.

The distant riverbank was pink. Approaching revealed a horde of flamingoes, crowding the swampy edge. Posting two crocodile watchmen, I waded into the warm current, but relaxing proved impossible. My submerged head filled with visions of razor-sharp jaws. Lather, rinse, repeat became lather, rinse, retreat. I felt a little cleaner, sort of.

I lunched with the tribal elders. Each had two wives who all cooked together. The menu never changed. We drank chai: black tea boiled with milk and sugarcane. We ate ugali: ground corn and millet pronounced, "Ooh golly." Ugali is eaten from a community pile with unwashed hands; this tends to darken the pile as the meal progresses. The grain paste is then used to scoop up beans or greens. "Greens" refers to any plant found round the hut that the goat missed or rejected.

Unfortunately I was an honored guest. A bowl of animal parts, suitable for teaching anatomy, was offered. I couldn't refuse. The assortment was a feast for a poor village. Starting with meats I recognized most and feared least, I commenced chewing. Bites lingered forever. Some refused decomposition and defied swallowing, but delicacies dwindled to two: a chunk of cerebral matter and a large intestine. Custom allowed leaving one. I visualized the gut section being squeezed out like a tube of brown toothpaste. "Brains it is!" I decided.

A woman entered. She was lean and hard like a runner, with movements soft and deft like a dancer's. High cheekbones cradled moist, glittering eyes. One silver and two wooden rings jangled around each wrist and ankle. She refilled our teacups. Instead of customarily exiting, she abruptly sat down. Tugging the straps from her arms, she let them fall away. Shoulders and breasts were exposed. I glanced furtively to gauge the elders' reactions; they seemed oblivious. Now, handed her baby, she began nursing. I slurped my tea.

My culture doesn't program people to feel passion for goat guts and passive about breasts—quite the opposite. Different societies install different life operating systems. As elders conversed, I pondered: to what extent can we choose to override or upgrade our own programming?

The finale was merseek: a sour, smoky drink of milk and charcoal fermented in a gourd. I quickly declined seconds. My hosts summoned me a matatu: a taxi/pick-up truck that appeared to be transporting about 100 people and their livestock at about 100 miles per hour. After a thrill-packed ride to Kisumu, I boarded the night train to Nairobi.

My cabin was clean. My berth had fresh, cinnamon-scented white linens. My sink oversaw the window. Brushing my teeth, I watched a fiery, red sun setting on savannah. Then darkness fell on the long silhouettes of giraffe munching treetops. I migrated to the brass and mahogany dining car. Sharing a table with a member of parliament, I ate chicken curry topped with coconut, bananas, peppers, and mango chutney. The train's rolling motion lulled me; the politician's voice sedated me. I slept deeply.

In Nairobi I slept with the Amish: Mennonites who ran a guesthouse: a secluded, garden oasis between a monastery and a spa. Bed, dresser, and bare walls with crucifix comprised a room. Rock floor, open sky, and flowering shrubs enclosed a shower. Each dawn, a clanging triangle rousted us staggering to breakfast: oatmeal porridge, milk, and guava juice.

Surrounding the table were bleary-eyed adventurers on a mutually bad hair day. The clinking of silverware and glasses gave way to the rising buzz of conversations. Blue napkins were encircled by hand-carved animal figurines. Mine was a zebra. Guests were permanently assigned to beasts. Sitting by our randomly distributed statuettes, every mealtime brought new acquaintances. One day's destiny paired me with a gray-bearded man. I spoke first: "Jambo, habari?"

"I'm all right, but I don't speak Kiswahili."

"So what brings you here?"

"I'm a bush doctor. I deliver babies and antibiotics."

"That sounds interesting."

"Oh yeah, great! Villagers pay the shaman to stuff their wounds with leaves. Then, broke and dying, they come to me. Gave up a lucrative practice in New York. Told my wife I wanted to help people and the bitch divorced me."

"The guava is delicious. Don't you think?"

"Everyone's driving out to the national park today. Wanna come?"

"Sure. Why not?"

Seven people piled into a beige Land Rover. Doc drove. Stomping the accelerator and scattering gravel, he took off like a kid for Disneyland. Multitasking as chauffeur and guide, his head spun recklessly from windshield to back seat. Hours passed. Dusty roads wound endlessly through saltbush and flat-topped acacia. Rounding a curve, we careened to a halt. Four stocky warthogs surrounded the business end of a long python. The meeting abruptly adjourned, waddling and slithering into the brush.

We crested a hill where a vast rift severed the landscape. Herds drifted lazily across the sea of stubble grass—massive wildebeest and delicate gazelles. We eagerly ploughed ahead, shifting gears and bouncing down a rock-studded hillside.

On the right, hyenas burrowed lustily into a pinkish-white carcass. On the left, a camouflage jeep passed by. Out of the window, fingers pointed and voices shouted, "Simba! Simba!" Adrenaline mounting, we approached the spot. There he was: flanked by two lionesses and lying under a tamarind tree, tufted tail and carpeted torso, rippling haunches and radiating mane. He yawned carelessly and stretched defiantly. I stared open-mouthed, very aware we had parked too close. My carpool mates furiously snapped photos, leaning out the windows, climbing on the roof. The lion looked annoyed. He stood, pawed the air, and snarled a warning. We headed home.

Somber gray skies set the mood for our drive. Storm clouds hung like sooty cotton balls as gentle thunder rumbled across the open range. Tall grasses rippled and bowed under the wind's unseen hand. We rode silently until roof-pattering rain filled the void. All was right until everything went wrong.

Our vehicle lunged downward and stopped cold. Cargo hurled forward. Left-side passengers flung right and introduced themselves. The engine shuddered, farted, and died. For a frozen moment, no one moved or spoke. We eyeballed each other till a resident genius said, "Musta hit somethin!" Sure enough, our tire had hit a deep rut.

Jumping out, we fanned around the freshly entombed wheel. Like a committee of experts we rubbed our jaws and performed a visual auto autopsy. Tire and rim had been yanked apart, the latter bent, the former mangled. A bumper-mounted winch offered some hope. Hooking cable to a tree, we pulled the SUV clear—only then discovering a flat spare.

We were stranded on a remote stretch with a bad reputation. If someone passed us (unlikely), and didn't rob us (less likely), they couldn't possibly transport us. Nothing to do but wait. We'd be found, either by Mennonites in a few hours or by archeologists in a few centuries.

Daylight faded out; insect noise faded in, as if Mother Nature simultaneously adjusted two knobs on her entertainment system. Long after dark, a distant car sound invaded the night. The guesthouse VW Bug appeared, beep-beeping a friendly "Hello." Seven plus driver squeezed in eagerly, as if sitting on another guy's lap, between an elbow and an armpit, was a rare treat.

A few head-bumping, bone-shaking kilometers later we stopped—some kind of checkpoint. Tire-puncturing spikes blocked half the road; more obstructions up ahead blocked the other half. We had to make a slow "S" maneuver. Two men in baggy green fatigues appeared from the brush. One fingered an AK-47; one shoulder-holstered a handgun. Both motioned us to halt.

"Handgun" looked us over, sneered, and spit on the ground. "AK-47" took a long puff, flicked the cigarette away, and challenged our driver: "You were speeding. Pay the fine!"

"I left home without any money."

"Gimme some identification!"

"I forgot to bring that, too."

Long pause. "Your registration sticker's expired. Get out of the car!"

They lined us up by a roadside ditch. My heart pounded with fear. They groped over our cameras and backpacks. My muscles tensed with readiness. They crossed the road, squabbling in tribal dialect. My mind raced with questions: Should I dash for the trees? Could I get everyone killed? Would the others bolt first?

Meanwhile, disagreement escalated. Their spat seemingly revolved around whether our gear merited the nuisance of shooting and burying us. I side-glanced accusingly at those who'd brought nicer wares. "AK-47" appeared to be on our side. (In other words, he thought our stuff was cheap.) I mentally cheered him on, but apparently "handgun" outranked him. I felt like a death-row inmate discovering his lawyer's a rookie.

Finally "AK-47" barked at us, "Get out of here!" "Handgun" threw down his weapon angrily. The silvery moon emerged from cloudbank, bathing us in milky light. A pee stain could be seen on Doc's pants. Scrambling to the VW, we dove in and drove off. Neither legs flailing out the doors nor a deflated rear tire slowed us down. I was grateful both to be alive and not to be sitting on Doc's lap.

The backseat was a jumble of people—not packed in like sardines, tossed in like salad. At first, personal space was established by self-conscious compression, but joints tired of assumed contortions; lungs rebelled against forced inhalations. Body parts sagged and settled, requiring counter-adjustments, and parts weren't just parts. The difference between boys and girls loomed before me like a puberty refresher course. Accidental brushes inspired outward courtesy and inward electricity. During such tactile collisions, my arm hairs bristled or recoiled, micro-flagging sexual preference. Stuck in this mobile game of twister, I retreated into my thoughts.

The roadblock incident bothered me. Being near death wasn't the problem—after all, I'm always a heartbeat away—facing death was the problem. I thrive on the perpetual self-delusion that death is inevitable but not imminent; the grim reaper can stand just outside the door as long as he doesn't knock. Nevertheless, to be human is to be trapped between the monkeys and the gods: too philosophical to live in the moment, too weak to secure immortality. My culture solves this dilemma by ignoring it. When that strategy fails, when reality is rubbed in my face, I freak out. Putting such heavy issues aside, I decided tomorrow I'd relax and escape by going to a movie.

Sunrise found me on a dust-blown airstrip in a battered Cessna suggesting more historical than aviational value. At takeoff, we were flung skyward and somehow stayed there. Looking surprised, the pilot beamed. My mouth hung loose in disbelief; I'd paid cash-money for this aerial reenactment of "The Little Engine That Could".

Riding air currents like surf, we sputtered to the crests and careened down. My green face stared longingly below where an elephant herd made slower, steadier progress. The fuel gauge heralded our arrival. I took deep breaths and made allegiance to several world religions. We landed.

The coastal port of Mombasa teems with commerce: Arab traders, Indian restaurateurs, and African prostitutes. I checked into a hotel. By afternoon, I was perusing a coral reef, submerged in soundless solitude. I told the fish I was a refugee from the upper world; they granted me temporary asylum.

By evening, I was sipping soda at the cinema. The smell of something burning went almost unnoticed. Behind me was a balcony; above the balcony was a ledge; on the ledge was a fan; with the fan was a cord; from the cord emitted sparks; the sparks ignited a flame; the flame started a frenzy.

I stood up to join the door-rushing throng. Suddenly, a theatre employee emerged on the ledge. Beating the fire to death with an old blanket, he disappeared. The movie resumed; the crowd sat down. Thirty minutes later, the whole scenario was repeated: fire, hubbub, blanket, film. Everyone stayed to the movie's end. (There are places where human life, unlike Hollywood footage, isn't a precious commodity.)

I stumbled out into the night—so far from home even the stars were different. My eye fixed on a pulsating constellation. Some long-ago sailor, finding a familiar symbol in a foreign sky, had named it "the Southern Cross." My heart was comforted. Like the corn grower, I knew there were life forces bigger than I; like the sea wanderer, I decided that was good.

Memoirs of a Samurai

"With this blade, you could circumcise a sleeping tiger."

My head nods. Taking the sword from Master Young, I succumb to the spell of the glistening steel arc. My heart pounds. The curved, single-edged Japanese Katana, crafted since the 8th century, is the finest cutting weapon ever made. My hands grip. A sharkskin hilt with a silk thread wrap gives a firm hold with a plush feel. My eyes scan. A cutout iron silhouette of warblers in a budding plum tree forms a hand-guard. A chiseled inscription records a quality test: "sliced diagonally through three criminal's torsos."

My mind studies. The flexible body has a wood-grain look from folding and hammering at the forge. The clay-hardened edge flashes a milky-white crystal configuration. My fingers grasp. A black-lacquered scabbard of fragrant wood sports a gold family crest. As the tip slides deep into the groove, the penetration is so sexual, my thoughts so readable, I flush.

I've come to Kyoto, Japan to learn kendo. Yet the ancient art of fencing is a punishing journey. Much sweat will fall before I wield a sharp blade again.

My training begins today. As I enter the dojo, Master Young silently glides across hardwood floor. He bows warmly. Only a silver streak on shiny black hair hints at his age. Every elegant move, from gravity-defying skyward leaps to heard-but-not-seen lethal swipes, speaks the unspoken but obvious: if he wasn't busy being wise, virtuous, and honorable, he'd kick your ass.

Few words pass his lips. I inquire whether to bring the bokken or shinai training sword to class. He responds with stern face and twinkling eyes, "Both, unless they are too heavy for you." I ask if my stance is correct. He answers, "Better, someday it will be correct." Fewer words now pass my lips.

The bokken is a heavy stick, shaped and balanced like a sword—standard equipment for solo practice since the 4th century. Legendary swordsman Musashi Miyamoto got so cocky and bored that he used one for some of his many deadly duels.

I hold the bokken improperly. Master Young positions me, tells me not to move, and walks off. I remain frozen as long as one can without permanent brain damage. He returns, presumably to rescue me. Instead, he adjusts my elbow, steps away, and flips open his cell phone—possibly consulting a retired master in his mountain retreat, possibly ordering a pizza.

I scope the room for distractions. Posted calligraphy engrains the warrior code of Bushido and expounds the philosophical roots of kendo. For example, Confucianism teaches that martial arts build a superior person. Daoism embraces the paradox of spirituality in harmony with warfare and offers the cosmic energy known to jedi as "the force" but to samurai as "ki." Shinto sees the spirits in natural elements. Thus a sword combines the spirits of earth iron, fire forging, and water quenching. Also, earth, fire, and water are the basic kendo fighting stances. Zen Buddhism aspires to merge the remaining elements of wind (my spirit), and the void (no-mindedness). I decide to draw inspiration from revered symbols of my own culture.

After I finish thinking about *Kill Bill*'s Uma Thurman, I try to completely empty my mind, like Tom Cruise in *Last Samurai*. This is hard. Having seen the actor in interviews, I suspect he has a natural gift for no-mindedness.

My muscles scream. As my body goes numb and Master Young's chat goes on, I focus all my mental energy on a single word, an ancient word, a word that cannot be written down—not because it is sacred, oh, no, quite the opposite!

Such bruising, exhausting sessions go on for months. Then comes the shinai. This bamboo and leather sparring tool neither looks nor feels like a real sword. The genius of the device is that practitioners can whack and smack to their heart's content and hardly anybody ever gets killed. Tradition suggests it was invented to save students from losing so many arms and legs. In light of the values of feudal Japan, perhaps it was more likely to spare the dojo floors from all that blood. (If medieval Japanese society were a chessboard, the pieces would be emperor, empress, priest, samurai, castle, and pawn.)

One day, a new prospective student shows up. There's something veeeeery different about this one. Oh yeah, she's a girl—bubblegum pumps, knee socks, purple with heather plaid skirt, hair twirled in her mouth, and Japanese ergonomics. All Master Young's admonitions about maintaining proper alignment and giving maximum effort suddenly take hold on the entire class. It's as if the blood has rushed from our brains into our swords—like a miracle from above … well, from somewhere.

As winter turns to spring, all lessons build to a defining moment: my first match. When the day comes, I carry myself deliberately, putting on my armor piece by piece, fondly, mystically. Stepping out onto the floor, I flex every limb in confirmation that my body is a reliable ally. Slowing my breathing and calming my spirit, I avoid my opponent's eyes till I'm sure they'll reflect more fear than mine. Then I verify.

We bow to each other. That's the respect he's due; that's all the consideration he's due. Within seconds, I hear and feel his primal yell, but I strike deep and I strike hard. I don't pause; I don't think. Overcoming a lifetime of personal-space conditioning, I drive into him and through him. With neither anger nor empathy, I try to carve him like wood and smash him like pottery. When it's done, I stand glassy-eyed like a lion over its kill. Re-cognizing him as human, I bow again.

Eventually, my apprenticeship draws to a close. The last evening is spent by a crystal-staircase stream at a floor table spread with barley miso soup, veggie maki-zushi rolls, buckwheat/yam soba noodles, grilled yakitori chicken skewers, cold clear saki and hot green tea. At bedtime, a blushing woman administers shiatsu massage to "free up the ki along my meridians." I'm unaware that my body has meridians (though a pair of jeans once proved I was developing an equator) and I'm unsure about ki. Soon, however, there's no doubt she's located both. After her laying on of hands, all I can say is, "I was blind, but now I ki." I belieeeeeve!!!

Next morning, I prepare to return home. Swordsmanship may not be the most practical asset for modern life. So what? Neither is my college degree. Plus, unlike that thing hanging on my wall, this accomplishment comes with some pretty cool shoulder muscles.

Fledgling samuraites have flocked to Kyoto for over a thousand years. By day, we parry across timeworn floors, striving to prove whose sword is longest. At night we loiter under cherry blossoms, seeking to grasp the mysteries behind a geisha's kimono (or at least get a look at them).

Undoubtedly, the samurai pilgrimage has changed. Muddy, perilous horse-treks home are replaced by Tokyo bullet train. Midway Mount Fuji seems more rest stop than sacred shrine. Still, passing the alpine icon moves me to reflection.

A picture of the surreal slope once adorned my childhood bedroom, having returned with my grandfather from war. One day, as I sat on his knee, he mumbled, "Your grandmother and I saved some money for your college." Oblivious to his message, I scurried off. Six months later, a stroke took him away.

My Grandpa, the illiterate son of a logging town, held grueling odd jobs all his life. Yet, somewhere between painter and custodian he banked enough cash to fund my master's degree. Never got to thank him. My first paycheck doubled his highest wage, but I'm still working to become half the man he was.

Arriving home from samurai school and passing his photo in the hall, I instinctively bow. Could swear his expression changed.

Freaks & Franks of Rembrandtville

I need wooden shoes like I need a wooden condom. Maybe less. Yet, here I am in Schiphol airport eyein' 'em, tryin' 'em, and buyin' 'em with every other globetrotting hillbilly. Why? Well, that goes back a few months to my arrival in The Netherlands.

My nonstop flight was also non-sleep. Four jolly Germans sitting behind me held a beer-and-song-athon, across the polar ice cap and well into EU airspace. I was jetlagged and oom-pah-pahed.

Spent my first day abroad sipping coffee at a café and staring bleary-eyed at a canal. I was devoid of feeling; my thoughts lacked content … except for the recurring image of those clunky Dutch clogs displayed in the terminal. Why do tourists buy them?

None of the locals around me had been shod by a carpenter. The neighborhood offered no blond braids, windmills, or daffodils. However, it did sport a prostitution info center, a masochistic leatherwear crafter, and a botanical garden with the world's oldest pot plant. This was Holland.

Most Hollanders live in the Randstad metroplex encompassing Amsterdam, Rotterdam, and The Hague—a long way from the tulip fields, a short distance from the annex where non-blond Anne Frank wrote before attending Nazi death camp.

The waiter brought a warm, flaky appelgebak; my fork became a shovel. Like many such eetcafes, this one had three tables occupied by the owner, some old men watching girls, and a paying customer: me.

The joint's actual business was, well, the joint. A passerby approached the owner, "Hoeveel is de best stof?" (How much is your best marijuana?) A transaction commenced.

The buyer had spiked green hair. A dried blood-trickle led to a giant safety pin piercing his bicep. He clutched a dog leash. Wearing the steel studded collar at the other end was not a pet but a person—more or less.

The dynamic duo sat at my table while the proprietor fetched the order. I wondered what to say. (Petting the doggie seemed out of the question.) "Excuse me," I ventured, "I couldn't help noticing that you have an enormous pin sticking through your arm. Doesn't that hurt?"

Seeming puzzled, he glanced down at the adornment as if noticing it for the first time. "Yeah, I guess it does … but I'm into that."

Next day, I woke refreshed and ready to explore. The Rijksmuseum occupied my morning. Richly hued Rembrandts exuded a somber golden light, casting an awed hush over the spectators. I, too, was stunned. My exposure to the Dutch Masters had been mostly confined to cheap cigar boxes. I associated Rembrandt with old, dark, stuffy pictures. Instead, frame after frame, a cultural revolution unfolded before my eyes.

I first approached "Jeremiah Lamenting the Destruction of Jerusalem." The canvas portrays a biblical story: a spiritual man going his own way as a besieged city burns. Perhaps the flames dance and spoils glitter so because the artist wasn't simply reading but remembering. You see, Rembrandt didn't just paint this drama; he lived it.

In the late 16th century, tolerance was barely a wacky new idea. Protestant iconoclasts fanned out from Antwerp, "cleansing" catholic shrines of images, sculptures, and paintings. Knives slashed tapestry. Hammers demolished marble. Graffiti proclaimed: "Thou shalt have no other gods before me."

In reprisal, the Duke of Alva's Spanish troops descended upon the Netherlands for bloody inquisition. Nine thousand were punished for heresy. Tongues were pierced with hot needles en route to the gallows. Bodies were drawn and quartered or broken on the wheel before being burned at the stake. Religious literature, arts, and discussions were banned.

Catholic commander Valdez attacked Rembrandt's soon-to-be hometown, Leiden, destroying his grandmother's mill. Grain and hay supplies were cut off; starvation and plague racked the city. Then, "miraculous" floods encircled the Spanish army, forcing retreat. Celebration of the deliverance became the town's annual fair. Paintings of Pharaoh's army drowning and Jesus distributing bread and herring were posted in the town hall, giving the event biblical significance. Into this city where art was a matter of life or death, with a Protestant family and Catholic relatives, Rembrandt was born.

I stood enthralled again. This time it was a selfportrait with a wild mane of curls, shadowy mystic eyes, and rebel-thug jaw. The dean of painters fancied himself James Dean. No doubt, he was a maverick. He portrayed himself wearing a beret at Jesus' crucifixion. He hung out with Protestants, Catholics, Mennonites, and Jews. He etched the Good Samaritan (a parable about compassion across ethnic and religious boundaries) with a mutt straining to take a dump in the lit foreground, reminding us that such lofty ideals are often crapped on.

He tolerated not only diverse ideas but also diverse humanity. He painted cellulite-riddled nudes sufficiently horrific to make any brush go limp. He etched squat-pissing women and stand-pissing men. He refused a study sabbatical in Italy, rejecting the sacrosanct notion that art must emanate from the classical tradition of platonic ideals. Instead, he found the divine in fish or cabbages and peopled his biblical narratives with earthy folks from the corner pub, holding forth pewter flagons of brew.

I gazed briefly at Rembrandt's "Portrait of Johannes Wtenbogaert," a persecuted crusader for religious tolerance, then "An Old Woman Reading Scripture," a classic study of the individual pursuing spirituality without hierarchy or tradition. A theme was becoming obvious. I mused over "The Stone Bridge," two pilgrims boating across a river leaving behind a church-spired horizon, followed by "Self-portrait as St. Paul," which collapses the boundary between saint and sinner, everyman and holy man, establishing sanctity within mere humanity.

I ogled the legendary "Night Watch." Except that it's not a "watch" (more of a jumble, a tumbling out of an archway), and it's not at "night" (the nocturnal impression comes from age-darkened varnish).

This portrait of Captain Frans Banning Cocq and his company of rowdy republic-defending militia broke all the conventions of posed, horizontal group pics in favor of a tribute to freedom even within organization. The work hung in a banquet hall where gentlemen soldiers celebrated their defense of the tolerant pluralistic marketplace that was Amsterdam.

A broad strip was cut off the painting's left side to make it fit the allotted space, resulting in a loss of contextual perspective. My kneejerk reaction was to brand this as cultural neanderthalism. However, paintings were a standard mass medium of the day. Such resizing was the equivalent of today's magazine editor reformatting an article to access a broader audience.

Maybe we moderns can still learn a thing or two about tolerating divergent ideas. No stranger to compromise himself, Rembrandt had actually stitched the "Night Watch" together from several canvasses. Perhaps we can also learn to tolerate our own patchwork lives, if not consider them masterpieces.

Nearly as famous is "The Sampling Officials of the Drapers' Guild." The disturbing gaze of the six men dressed in black—two Catholics, a Calvinist, a Mennonite, an ecumenical, and a steward—pulls you into the gathering and poses the question: if differing beliefs can coexist to make a buck, why not for other reasons?

Congealing profound concepts like tolerance into easily overlooked compositional details is the Rembrandt way. Take, for example, the "Portrait of Jan Six." This mind-blowing work combines minute detail painting and loose impressionistic strokes into a unified living presence beyond any other 17th century work. The painting captures an aristocratic friend in the act of donning or removing gloves. His hands are a blur of optical-illusionist movement. In that age of social pretensions, the picture dared to reveal both Jan's public and private worlds.

The façade-busting Rembrandt yearned for tolerance that was not so much the freedom to believe as the freedom to live what you be. He hungered for this not just in the pursuit of truth (a dubious concept to many moderns), but also in the pursuit of sanity, of wholeness, of replacing cognitive dissonance with an integrated self.

My last canvas to peruse, "The Jewish Bride," was no less weighty but aimed more at the heart. A young husband gently places his hand over his wife's breast as she reassuringly reinforces it with her own, while her other hand hovers over her womb and their heads incline toward each other. Even after losing his wife to tuberculosis, his house to bankruptcy, his reputation to critics, and his son to the plague, Rembrandt never stopped celebrating the abundance and fertility of life.

His own progeny possibly includes our free society itself. Vincent Van Gogh would one day stand on the same spot I occupied, awestruck before that same canvas. As Rembrandt often dared to make himself the model, so Van Gogh would dare to make himself the subject, and eventually our bistro bicep-piercer would make himself the canvas.

In the rented house on the Rozengracht where Rembrandt was found dead, a few meager possessions remained, including an unfinished "Return of the Prodigal Son." This painting of a man devastated by his folly coming home to his father (symbolizing God) suggests the artist never surrendered his lifelong obsession that both imperfect ideas and flawed humans have a right to exist and even find grace.

Exiting the museum, I found my way to a table, a Heineken, some Gouda, and more reflection. I had no doubt our world still has much to learn about tolerance. Back home the streets are filled with classically sculpted bodies that nevertheless can't accept themselves without multiple cosmetic surgeries.

Intolerance toward neighbors also runs rampant. Many Americans proclaim "all men are created equal" but support border-security racial-profiling, suggesting that, on the capitalist plantation like the Orwellian farm, "some are more equal than others." Many Canadians smugly eschew bigotry and hate-speech while booing American children at Quebec sporting events and electing to parliament the self-professed American-hater Carolyn Parrish. Many Natives decry prejudice then summarize past deeds of some Europeans with the maxim: "the whites took our land," just as Nazis twisted ancient acts of a few into the mantra: "the Jews killed Jesus."

We must be tolerant both of others and ourselves to nurture the freedom Rembrandt espoused yet Anne Frank was denied. This includes the sacred right to green hair and a leash. A free society is a rich tapestry, but this tapestry always has a fringe. While bicep pins offer negligible benefit, other weird ideas turn out to be brilliant. Freedom allows both deviation and innovation. Such innovation has lifted many out of hunger and superstition.

Thus "freaks" occupy a necessary niche in my worldview. Still, how could I explain this broadmindedness acquired abroad to my mother at home? I couldn't. What, then, of my commitment to being a traveler who travels to experience the real world rather than a tourist who tours to escape the same? Must truth-in-travel-reporting include shattering mom's Hollandish pipe dreams with hashish pipe nightmares? Surely not. How many times had mother gently preserved my toddler delusion that perverse crayon stylings were actually artistic wonders?

Anne Frank once confessed a great liking for art, poets, and painters but a great loathing for Algebra, Geometry, and figures. She must have loved her co-romantic, Rembrandt, who bathed a harsh world in warm embracing light. Stark realities must be viewed, of course, but a soft lens sometimes comes in handy.

Frankly (and Rembrandtly), the more I pondered, the more attractive those wooden shoes became. In fact, giving mom a little peace of mind and some nifty coffee-table décor, all for a few Euros, was really quite a bargain.

Moldy Socks & the Three Bears

As with Goldilocks, my bear encounters are always too cold or too hot.

When I was a kid, my dad took me backpacking in California (a state officially symbolized by a grizzly) at Yosemite (a Native word for grizzly), following trail markers of Smoky (a cartoon grizzly) through an area long devoid of grizzlies. Nevertheless, I lay awake all night waiting for Ursus Horribilis to appear and eat my father, an event that my childish mind expected to be both heartbreaking and cool to watch. Instead, we encountered a black bear so used to campers that he could light a barbeque grill and make sign language for "Please, no onions on the hot dogs, folks; they give me wind."

Recently, while hiking the Kootenays, the first blood-curdling growl came from a distant chainsaw; the second came from my girlfriend's stomach; however, the third came from a cave guarding the only escape off the rock ledge we were scaling. Perhaps I should start at the beginning.

Landing in Castlegar, I sucked in mountain air and gawked at an elk herd grazing just beyond the runway. A black flyrod case hung on my right arm while a brunette flight attendant hung on my left. (Some days are definitely better than others.) We drove a rental car past a cliff-hugging caravan of bighorn sheep to the Slocan River. Highway 6 shot us North through the narrow valley cradling this gently looping, translucent-green glacial melt. Arrived in Passmore at lunchtime.

Three stout Russian Doukhobor sisters served us borscht and rye bread. They were seamstresses specializing in wedding dresses and coffin linings. Not as eclectic as it may seem. When the pacifist Christian Doukhobors fled Czarist persecution to Canada a century ago with the help of Leo Tolstoy, they came espousing communal landholding and the withholding of communal data, like marriages and deaths, from the government. Our sewing siblings also explained how female forebears had fished the Slocan using only their headscarves.

Back on the road, we soon stopped for gas at a co-op near Vallican. Unexpectedly, a glitter-and-rainbow van lurched down the forested hillside, jolted over the concrete embankment, and pulled up to a pump. A scraggly-bearded driver in tie-dyed shirt and overalls hopped out. I asked him curiously, "Why didn't you use the road?"

He answered matter-of-factly, "I don't have a license." To those who know the Slocan's history, this almost makes sense.

In 1846, The Oregon Treaty extended the 49th parallel border to the Pacific. Slocan area residents, of course, were neither consulted nor considered. Yet, their lives were forever changed. Relatives and trading partners along the North and South Columbia River were arbitrarily divided into Canadians and Americans. Strangers beyond the uncrossable Eastern and Western mountains became their countrymen and overseers. Furthermore, the Columbia River highway, which allowed BC surveyor Gilbert Malcolm Sproat to describe the Kootenays as nearly "the most accessible region in the province," was blocked off. The Slocan literally became a backwater.

Ever since, residents have had a tendency to take legislation from afar with a grain of salt (or even a pinch of marijuana). Thus, when hordes of draft-dodging American hippies showed up in the 1970s, establishing communes and fishing the Slocan with willows, few eyebrows were raised.

Slocanites are a law-abiding people, but there is some confusion in the valley as to whose laws they are abiding. Local ways often prevail.

In Winlaw we had dinner at the Hungry Wolf Café. Ate too much, too fast. After this big bad wolfing, what could be more appropriate than for us little pigs to retire to a straw house? Actually, it was a dome-shaped straw-bale-construction house and things got totally inappropriate.

The owner was a fortyish Scandinavian free spirit. She wore Daisy Duke shorts and a bikini top, behind which her unbridled she-appendages galloped like wild horses as she bounced around before us and sprawled across her unmade bed. The advertised B&B turned out to be the room she occupied, where we were enthusiastically informed the three of us could share everything. Driving away, I pondered kinky stuff B&B could stand for, while my airline honey harangued me in her native French for taking 1.6 seconds too long rejecting the threesome concept.

Our road veered sharply upward. Cedar, fir, hemlock, and pine punctuated a left-side view of the valley floor receding to dizzying depths. A hairpin turn offered a near-fatal panorama of a timber mill operating far below. Slocan Lake then appeared. This stringbean-shaped pool is 28 miles of bull trout and kokanee, surrounded by maples and cottonwoods, wedged between the granite flanks of the Selkirk Mountains. The jagged Valhalla Range lies to the West with the undulating Slocan Range to the East. My mind slipped into a state akin to worship.

In Silverton we rented a cabin. The immaculate log home, owned by Swiss "healing-crystal-importers," housed the cast of Snow Falling On Cedars during filming. A fitting location for an Anglo-Asian tragedy. In 1942, politicians chose this valley to hide away over 7,000 Japanese Canadians who had been herded into livestock pens at Vancouver's agricultural exhibition lot after having their possessions confiscated.

Here, future environmentalist David Suzuki saw tall trees through a child's eyes. Here, Dr. Hiroshi Kamitakahara healed patients and fished with a bamboo rod. Here, they waited for their country to decide they were no longer a wartime security threat and for jealous neighbors to decide they were no longer a hard-times economic threat. My heart slipped into a state akin to shame.

The next day I went angling in New Denver. Straddling a gravel bar, I worked my graphite rod back and forth, pushing a hand-tied sculpin farther and farther over the chilly abyss. My sinking line repeatedly pierced the realm where monsters be, but leviathans of the deep paid no heed.

Over 200 meters down, miners had once lost a boxcar full of silver. I figured if I were lucky enough to snag a bar of bullion, the Department of Fisheries and Oceans would likely make me throw it back. Prospectors also fished this spot—with dynamite. I decided to retain a little dignity and go with a dry fly instead. Good call. I unrolled my floating line down the shallows like a reptilian tongue, but instead of snatching an insect, planted a black stonefly between thick bulrushes and a dead log, like pizza delivery to the home of Mr. And Mrs. Kokanee. Several catches later, I paused for a bite myself.

On this particular day, I was practicing the highest form of angling: catch and release into a skillet full of butter. Drank one Kokanee Beer for each kokanee salmon to maintain essential carb/protein balance. Right away, a slightly overcooked fish on the edge of the pan spoke. No, really. I bent down next to his charred body (sort of like that scene in The English Patient), as he confided a longing for his lost Pacific cousins beyond those Columbia River dams.

Now, two things occurred to me hunched over listening to that frying fish: 1) my hair smells kind of funny when it catches fire and 2) we should probably give rivers more of the protection they give us. From Doukhobors fleeing political persecution to suburbanites fleeing spousal criticism, rivers have always offered refuge. Plus, from East Coast Celts to West Coast Natives, we're descended from people who listen to rivers, so why not a talking fish?

Somewhere back in the mists of time, Native fishermen paddled into this remote valley and called it "Slocan" or "place of bull trout." I, too, had ventured in and reported a fair amount of bull. Nevertheless, I write this in earnest: police cars gather and news copters circle when urban freeways snarl up for minutes, so maybe it isn't extreme to note the long-term blockage of the arterial waterways draining our continent or even to hope that someday these emerald currents will flow again unhindered to the sea.

At sunrise, mademoiselle and I stood on the Slocan Lake shore. Shining waters lapped against our boots. On the opposite side, an ancient aboriginal painting adorns the sheer rock face ascending from the glossy deep; thick red ochre portrays an enraged bear accosting two people. History would soon repeat itself.

We set off along Carpenter Creek to Sandon. This ghost town lies in a crevasse prone to wildfire in summer, avalanche in winter, and a minute or two of sun each day. Still, thousands once lived here. Why? Because silver-bearing galena ore was thrust up on the site 140 million years ago. Then, American Jack Seaton and Frenchman Eli Carpenter stumbled onto it in 1891. The bonanza was on; the partnership was off.

From Sandon, we hiked up Idaho Peak. A weathered forestry watchtower creaked in the summit wind while mountain ranges wrinkled away as far as the eye could see. I was awestruck. In such a place, the myth of human importance erodes faster than any structure. Coming back down into thick brush, we heard heart-stopping bear sounds—some bogus, some real. One thing I've learned from bears is to keep my distance from other large predators, which we did.

(By the way, you can learn a lot from bears. Ursine biologist Greg Risdahl tells me that they adapt not just winter hibernation but also summer snoozes to their environment. Sleeping by nature's rhythms can help people, too. Remember "early to bed, early to rise, makes you healthy, wealthy, and wise"? Think about it. Natural lighting fights infection and depression, dawn rising promotes early bird productivity rather than night owl consumption, and sunrise watching fosters a spiritual sense of one's niche in the world. Yes, only geeks go to bed early, but healthy, wealthy, wise geeks can seem pretty hip.

Risdahl also points out that bear and human teeth reveal natural diet. Molars and premolars are for grinding grains, fruits, vegetables, legumes, and seeds—not milled flour, fruit juices, veggie bars, soy milks, and oil blends. Waste not, want not. Canines and incisors are for tearing lean meat such as venison or trout, not fat-packed sausage or pre-ground hamburger. Bears who trade forageable fare for human-processed garbage suffer ill health. Ditto for people. In Tolstoy's *War and Peace*, Count Bezukhov credits his transformed vitality to meeting a man so close to nature he is part of it. We're all part of nature and we're all omnivores. Meat lovers attempting to live as carnivores risk stroke and heart disease; vegetarians attempting to live as herbivores risk atrophy and diabetes. Respecting nature means embracing its blueprint and accepting our place in it.)

We spent the rest of the afternoon trekking across ridges and ravines to an ethereal blue glacier. Sat too long by the glowing ice field, till dusk began to fall. Alas, the dumbest word in all of wilderness travel, "shortcut," was uttered and agreed upon. Leaping from boulder to boulder checkerboard style, we advanced down an old rockslide, barely arresting our momentum at a precipice. Peering over the edge, I watched a steady stream of gravel trickling into oblivion, like the blood draining from my face.

We crawled sideways along the lethal dropoff till reaching another dead end. Our only way out was back up the long descent with an alpine night fast approaching. As we turned to face this lone dismal option, a previously unseen hole in the rocks transformed gloom into horror. A territorial growl began as a low rumble.

I was quite sure my lovely companion would smell tasty to a bear; I only hoped my hiking socks would neutralize the appeal. Looking around for ideas, I saw nothing but fresh berry-laden scat. Grrrrrrr! I trembled visibly and whined softly, "Oh ursus … oh Jesus … oh help us!"

If I'd been cad enough to try out-running the agile Kimberly-Marie, I couldn't have. If I'd been chivalrous enough to lay down my life, she'd simply have been left on that stone pantry-shelf for a later meal. There was nothing to do but inch our way up to and beyond the den mouth. With each noise, we froze. Otherwise, we moved at approximately the speed of tree growth in a desperate attempt to give the grizzly no particular motion worthy of a charge. After what seemed like only a year or two, we were safely away.

That night, I discovered Kimberly-Marie was not just physically fit; she knew her astronomy too. As we lay down to sleep under the stars, she exclaimed passionately, "Uranus is cold and surrounded by gases!" To show respect for her expertise, I commented, "I've met only a few women who respond with such enthusiasm to a heavenly body." Her expression was confusing, but I guess space buffs are an odd bunch. She insisted we leave.

As I drove off toward Kaslo, an enormous bear lumbered onto the road before us, moseying obliviously down the middle at an excruciatingly slow crawl with his glorious backside lit up in my headlights. Well, that's the end. Quite a tale. No buts about it, I was really bummed. Guess when it comes to grizzlies, hindsight is always better than …

Losing My Religion

Much of my life is a quest to answer a question. If, as so many of us believe, you don't have to be religious to be spiritual, what do you have to be? I can pinpoint the moment this obsession began: an old woman passed me some strawberry jam then burst out, "We goes to a real nice church, and I ain't meanin' that nigger church!" Let me explain.

I was nineteen and walking across Arkansas. Why? Sort of a sample the simple life kind of thing, like Paris Hilton without the funds. I wore a T-shirt, jeans, and backpack. My weather forecast was way off; a churning sky looked ugly and angry. As raven-hued cloud-mass cracked open and hailed, I ducked inside a church. Instantly, every eye was on me. The pews were white; the members were not.

Worship reignited when Reverend King broke into rhyme: "On one side of town, folks drivin' Cadillacs; on the other side of town, folks havin' heart attacks; all over town, folks need to know the facts. Jeeesus is my A; all I ever need. Jeeesus is my B; beautiful to see …"

Yes, he made it all the way to Z, without missing a beat, and (taking a cheap shot at Arkansas) without missing a letter. The room was small; the crowd was large (and numerous). "Da King" started dancing, the audience started stomping, and everybody started sweating. We sang "Amen" over and over, until all dripping bodies meshed arm in arm into a swaying trance.

Afterwards, people dispersed. Every visitor was invited to someone's house for supper—except the one lone white guy, who almost got his groove back. A rucksack suddenly seemed heavier.

Next morning—across the railroad tracks, on the other side of town, with country music playing, over ham, eggs, and biscuits—I sat in stone silence as the guesthouse owner offered up her religion and even less subtle racism.

With a bruised but resilient soul, I struck out across the cotton fields. The scenery was like a page ripped from John Grisham's *A Painted House*. A rising sun lit up the dewdrops, chasing away my darker thoughts. Abruptly, I came across a blazing red cardinal flopping on the ground. Clasping her in hand, I unsnagged a thorn from the left wing. The tiny breast heaved up and down as her racing heart threatened to explode. I released her to hop, hop, and fly away. Little did she know that my heart was also endangered, or that she had restored my spirit's ability to fly.

Looking upward, I addressed an audible "Thanks" to the general management.

Ever since that day, I've preferred to take my spirituality with as little religion as possible. Unfortunately, that's not the way it's usually served.

Years later, I stumbled into a very different church. Its stained glass and Celtic symbols had graced the British Columbia skyline since 1891. To the right was a Tudor-style pub serving up cheap breakfast; to the left was a used-condom-and-hypodermic-needle-studded park with a floral wreath marking a recent murder site; across the street was the Elizabeth Fry Society, providing shelter for women in transition from drugs, beatings, prostitution, and incarceration. I ascended steep granite steps as a man in black shirt and white collar extended a pink fleshy hand.

The lobby featured framed scrolls listing members living, dead, and (being Presbyterian) somewhere in-between. Campbell, McDonald, McKnight—I was just catching on to the ethnic trend when a guy strode past me sporting a red ponytail and kilt.

After worship, everyone gathered in the fellowship hall for strawberry tea and Scottish shortbread. (I was reminded of the Arkansas jam and that the English even call these cookies biscuits.) Most of the congregation were either elderly men or divorced moms, and I met one of each. A flustered but aggressive woman downloaded on me the many reasons she hated her ex, whom she described as a "typical male." Then, after reciting her vast martial arts pedigree, she explained in bone-crunching detail what she'd do to any man who tried to assault her.

Weary from assuming submissive, non-threatening postures, I sat down by a white-haired, soft-spoken member of my own gender. He began talking. Most of what he said was enjoyable until he landed on the subject of "those damn Americans." When he paused for air and asked me where I was from, I swallowed hard and mumbled, "California." Long awkward silence. For the first time in my life, I fully appreciated the need for brightly lit exit signs in public buildings.

Sometimes church sucks. Most people know this, so my dose of bad religion may not seem like divine epiphany, but God often speaks to the individual like a Horse Whisperer as well as to the multitudes from thundering Sinai. Frail and nervous humans and horses can be startled rather than guided by a booming voice. The soft glow of the exit marker was all the light from above I needed.

Glancing back as I descended the outside church stairs, I couldn't help thinking that the snow-capped mountains looked far more inspiring than the bronze-capped steeple. For thousands of years, lofty peaks and alpine forests filtered sunlight and inspired awe without the coordinated effort of stained glass. I saw little reason why they should not continue to do so.

My Big Fat Bulgarian Orgy

If you liked that movie, you'll hate this tale, because this is for guys and the only wedding here is the marriage of food, wine, music, and a voracious hottie. However, if the way to your heart is through your stomach, plus a nearby appendage, keep reading.

I arrived in the capital Sofia with twenty-four hours to relax. Took a taxi to the Bulgarska Zavera Restaurant on Tsar Samuil Street. The old masonry and walnut wood interior was covered with rifles and military paintings from the 1853 Crimean War. My table sat beneath a tea-urn once used by the Russian General Gurko, who liberated the country from the Ottoman Empire. (Wait a minute. Didn´t Luke Skywalker free everyone from the Ottoman Empire when he dropped the bomb into that thingy? Maybe I´m confused.)

A waitress bent over me, pouring red wine and revealing creamy cleavage. I blurted out "Thanks" a bit too enthusiastically. The meal began with a shopska salad of tomatoes, cucumbers, peppers, onions, olives, parsley, and white cheese. Next came a cold Tarator soup with yogurt, cucumbers, nuts, and dill—way better than it sounds. Finally, a steaming platter arrived. Rack of pork was roasted on a traditional iron pan with onion, pepper, eggplant, carrots, olives, mushrooms, potatoes, and bacon. The second-most-delicious-looking rack I'd seen that night fully satisfied. After a good bit more wine, I staggered down to Pirotska Street and crashed at the Hotel Sveta Sofia.

At sunrise, I stepped onto the balcony to find myself surrounded by rustic-tiled roofs and snowcapped mountains. The air was cool and fresh. I felt that common traveler's sentiment: I could probably live here. Hopped into the shower. As I was soaping up and rinsing off, the cleaning staff decided to go the extra mile, which was about ten feet too far. Turning off the water and pulling aside the curtain, I discovered that someone had come in while I was naked and placed a towel within arms reach. They had also made the bed.

If I said I was generally opposed to nude encounters with strangers, I'd be lyin' big time. Nor did I feel violated like most women would. I just felt she should have made her presence known, so I would have had the option to ask her to wait outside or to ask her to do something completely inappropriate. Instead, she carried out her duties routinely—almost as if this wet, writhing hulk of masculine flesh exerted no gravitational pull on her whatsoever. Needless to say, I was deeply offended.

Since it was Sunday morning, I opted to check out the Alexander Nevski Cathedral. The ambiance was not unexpected: vast space between checkerboard marble floors and stained-glass-illuminated domes. The glowing chandeliers and rich incense were also familiar. However, the hour-long musical conversation between the lofty ringing choir and the ZZ Top-bearded chanting priests can only be described as skin-tingling, soul-stirring Gothic opera.

Almost as stunning as the moment the music began was the moment when it stopped. The people crowded forward together to receive sacred bread—not translucent wafer but marketplace bread, not one holy relic that must be guarded but an overflowing two hands full of pieces that begged to be shared. Perhaps an equally worthy view of grace. I gave the shadowy cavernous room a last perusal. Rows of iconic portraits, framed by peacock and grapevine laden arches on columns, were astonishing. Yet, the eye candy was nothing compared to the inescapable feeling elicited that there is one artist and architect above all others. Let's just say I gave the show a two-thumbs-up and leave it at that.

Walking away from the cathedral, I immediately passed a strip club called Taboo, where I assumed less ancient heavenly forms were inspiring awe. Maybe, in a spirit of ecumenicism, I should have joined those worshipers, too. Maybe not.

Instead I stopped at a coffee house with the incredibly accurate and helpful name "Coffee House." I once asked a wise old lady "Which is better: coffee or women?" She retorted, "Both are delicious, but the coffee won't cause you much trouble." What could the oracle at Delphi have possibly offered to top that? Fortunately, I didn't have to choose. As I sipped my java, five-plus feet of curves and hair, wearing sexy librarian glasses, plopped down at the closest table. Apparently Eastern Orthodox prayers are the most effective. Since my camera wasn't working, I took it out and melodramatized the problem until she offered to help. Soon we were exchanging email addresses and making rendezvous plans.

Time for lunch. Drifting through the neighborhood, I stumbled into Cookie's Bar and Café. The velvet curtains, chrome pillars, paper lanterns, and hardwood furnishings had both a chic and yesteryear quality that was instantly relaxing. The impossibly-tight blue jeans worn by my statuesque server were instantly not relaxing. I foreplayed with a tabbouleh salad of Bulgar wheat, parsley, tomato, lemon peel, and olive oil, then climaxed on duck julienne with pretentious-but-delicious aromatic herbs including salvia, chamomile, and linden. Basking in the afterglow, I pretended to stare out the bay windows but checked out the fashionistas dining windowside. So, that's what they were hiding behind the iron curtain: really hot babes!

Spent the rest of the afternoon strolling through the big central market called Hali. It's like a mall full of Bulgarian hams, sausages, cheeses, breads, wines, beers, and salads like Fava beans in tomato dill sauce. Bought just about everything that might survive a suitcase.

Walking back on the darkening streets, I encountered the unmistakable sound and smell of blues and barbecue. Followed them down a crumbling alley. What I found was a party composed of hippie, gypsy, and mafioso types. The brown sandals, gray ponytails, and black leather jackets encircled me for a few wary questions before handing me a bottle of Zagorka Beer. I gratefully sat down.

The birthday bash was for Bulgaria's original and most famous blues player "Vasko the Patch." Grabbing his guitar and harmonica, he launched into a mournful groove he had recently written called "The Dark Side of the Wall." For a couple hours and a few brews, I was mesmerized by his tunes of woe and tales of freedom from communist oppression. The happenings ended with Vasko and me bellowing out Muddy Waters' classic "Hootchie Kootchie Man" together. Then he engaged in the greatest act of hospitality one man can show another: he introduced me to his loveliest and horniest friend.

You may hear that Bulgaria is a poor country devoid of amenities. I must admit I found little there except succulent food, tasty wine, soulful music, and attractive women. Still, I somehow muddled through.

The Winter of Our Content

An Internet site that described Zihuatanejo as "a small fishing village just south of Ixtapa" was packed with stunning photos, but what can I do here for a whole week, I wondered. The pirate Francis Drake once parked in this cove to keep an eye out for Spanish booty. "Well, shiver me Freudian timber!" I quipped, "Sounds like a plan."

My rental condo had a beach view from the window and a pizza delivery sticker on the fridge. Damn near paradise in my book. The décor was typical tropical: Casablanca fans and terra cotta tile, mahogany closets and calla lily sofa. I'd stocked the kitchen with papaya, yogurt, oats, and beer—all part of a complete breakfast. As the sun rose over banana trees, I headed out for a stroll along the surf.

With sandals dangling from my hand and foam swirling around my feet, I pondered the many historic footprints that had been made and erased on this spot. Doctor Timothy Leary conducted psychedelic LSD experiments here in 1963. Author Zane Gray caught a 135-pound world record sailfish here in 1924.

Still, I was more intrigued by the countless, nameless indigenous lovers who had no doubt left their marks on this lunar-powered etch-a-sketch, where every night the silvery moon draws hearts together then draws waves to obliterate all tracks. The very name Zihuatanejo stems from the Aztecan language Nahuatl and means "place for women." Nothing says amorous rendezvous like a beach.

In my past wanderings up the Pacific, I'd seen the coconut-strewn crescent bays of Huatulco and the dope-smoking nude surfers of Zipolite. What could be so special here? I rounded a promontory and there she was, sitting on a tidal rock, squeezing water out of long dark hair.

I asked her name. Chocolate eyes sparkled and native cheekbones flushed, but the voluptuous lips said nothing. (Generally in Mexico, guys are expected to show a little more effort; what Gringos call stalking, Latinos call unrequited love.) Pleasantly shitfaced, I tested a ridiculous line, "I know you're Azteca, but I hope you won't rip out my heart."

She didn't even blink, "I know you're Americano, but I hope you won't invade my territory." I grinned sheepishly; she laughed playfully. Five minutes later, we were conversing as friends. When a pelican dove for something eye-catching by the water and crashed headlong, I was relieved that his fate apparently wouldn't be mine.

As the breeze changed direction and came in off the ocean, I sensed the fresh wind a beautiful woman can usher into your life. The next few days were as perfect and hazy as those rock islands shimmering across the turquoise bay. We swam offshore for hours, talking and fucking to the rhythmic shoves and tugs of the sea.

Waves are the music of the planet. Combined with the polar magnetism of boy meets girl, they constitute a primal symphony. Art is the pursuit of beauty. Hand led by a bikinied silhouette into a shining ocean, one transcends mere hedonism for an earthly apprenticeship in the heavenly forms.

Alas, I've metamorphed from a normal guy into a wannabe poet. Blame the tropics. While the northern turning leaves mark the passing of years and urge productivity, the southern rolling waves hint of changeless eons and instill contentment. Whatever my future might bring, I was satisfied just to be there and seize that day.

She and I now live in different worlds—worlds forever different from each other, as well as from what they were before we met. Whenever I stroll the coastline of any ocean, the breakers seem to emanate from a distant shore, a shore where my Azteca forever sits on a tidal rock.

57

Pirates/Terrorists of the Caribbean

This ain't about some disneyfied, mascara-laden Johnny Dep flick. Nor is it a crusty ol' sea tale with Russell Crowe in ponytail. We're talking real buccaneers. I mean rum-guzzlin', gun-totin', swashbucklin' scoundrels, holed-up in the remote port of Punta Gorda, Belize. That's Spanish for "fat bitch point." On most maps, it's an empty spot above Honduras—not a completely inaccurate description. Yet that's where the scurvy little mates (plus the war-on-terrorism's dirty little secret), can be found. I four-wheeled through mangrove swamps to get there, spent two violent months there, and barely made it out of there. So, if you've got the time, I've got the nonfictional narrative.

I should've known Belize was different from day one. Make that day zero. Before entering the country, I visited the consulate in Chetumal, Mexico. I rang the office bell … rang the bell … rang the damn bell. The diplomat eventually appeared. His face was Latin; his hair was African; his accent was British. No surprise there: that's Belize. He wore black wool trousers, a puka shell necklace, and no shirt. That was different.

Crossing the Rio Hondo into Belize, I parked at customs. A motley crew, sporting filthy Bob Marley shirts and bogus ministry-of-tourism badges, gang-swarmed me—a con artists' convention. I declined all offers to carry and/or pilfer my bag. Most of my attending entourage then revealed their true identities as Reverend so-and-so of the Lord's such-and-such, thinking perhaps I preferred donating to tipping.

"No, leave me alone!" I screamed in my mind. "Argh, avast ye scalawags, afore I run ye through!" Actually, I offered them "go-away" coins. They scowled at the mere pittance, threw it on the ground, and stomped off.

I got in line at immigration. Apparently, Belize's no-extradition policy is quite good for tourism. I can't say the inbound crowd looked like pirates; they wore no peg legs or eye patches. However, scarf-bound stubs and scar-tissued sockets were everywhere. I can't say tattoos were everywhere; no floral etchings nestled in the butt-cracks ahead of me. Yet countless biceps recalled one of the world's military or penal institutions. Coincidentally, everyone had just come from visiting their aunts in New York, Miami, or Bogotá.

Suffice it to say, I didn't push or cut in line. If others did, well, I let them. Sometimes, I apologized or thanked them. My writer's motto: "Dead men tell no tales."

I finally reached the window. A delirious official stamped passports like a carny taking tickets. Ka-chunk, ka-chunk, ka-chunk: admit one to the wild Belize ride; hang on to your valuables.

Returning to the truck, I sped off. Rust-orange dirt road cut through drab-green bush country where prehistoric frigate birds navigated the seaward sky. Sweat dripped constantly into my eyes, except when I arm-wiped or shook it off.

I lunched in breezy Corozal. An oceanside market offered the standard Belizean fare: red beans and rice with coconut. I poured on the standard Belizean condiment: Marie Sharp's orange-habanero-pepper sauce. The bottle says "medium hot." That means "halfway between Creole and Hell." Once you try it, other peppers are only suitable as baby binkys.

Strolling the turquoise water's edge, I watched West Indian Manatees bobbing shyly. Nicknamed "sea cows," their appearance suggests a mermaid and a walrus committed unspeakable acts then birthed children. Bloated and wrinkled, they hover between lovable and laughable, cute and homely.

Back on the Northern Highway, I turned on the radio. Three choices: static, reggae, or no-holds-barred legislative proceedings. For a while, I enjoyed steel drums with voices extolling love, God, and marijuana. Then I dabbled in politicians questioning their colleagues' sanity, sobriety, and paternity.

Orange Walk gradually rose over the horizon. Rolling into the busy farming town, I fell behind a horse-drawn wagon loaded with sugarcane. Two men drove. Their hair and eye colors matched their straw hats and blue denim. They were Mennonites, part of a pacifist clan that fled Canada, shunning military service.

That's understandable. What conscientious person wouldn't rather raise a family surrounded by poachers, pirates, marauders, and mayhem than serve a stint with the bloodthirsty killers of the Canadian armed forces, defending a country so brutal as to amass a current weapons arsenal approximately that of the average LA rap artist? On second thought, maybe they were a tad hasty.

Whinnying and snorting, the horses clomped to a stop. No hint of pirates in this pastoral scene, I thought. Suddenly, the brethren left-turned their sweet cargo into a rum distillery. Yo, ho, ho!

The drive to Belize City was hypnotic. Monarch butterflies flitted in the sun-drenched air; boa constrictors slithered across the well-paved road. I reached the ramshackle, pirate-founded sprawl by dinnertime. Took the swing bridge across Haulover Creek to Albert Street. Parked and walked to Macy's Restaurant.

The special of the day was gibnut. Locals swear visiting Queen Elizabeth II loved this delicacy, until learning it was the huge rodent, paca. My thoughts transitioned inexplicably from visiting queens sucking on gibnuts to the male tourists cuddling at the opposite table. We conversed. One was a graying executive at a San Francisco utility company. The other was his young intern.

The elder handed over his camera, asking me to photograph them. His partner recoiled from such hard documentation of their romantic escapade. Getting hot-and-bothered by this coyness, the exec tickled the intern out the door into a car. Though the couple didn't strike me as swarthy sea-rogues, I had a strange premonition some booty was about to be plundered.

At dawn, I put my key to the ignition, but something made me pause. In the rearview mirror, sunrise over the sea looked like a juicy orange on a glass table. Belizean oranges are the juiciest. Nearly inedible, their thick, fibrous segmentations burst with liquid sunshine. A fresh-squeezed jug-for-the-road had just cost me pennies.

In front of me, the Western Highway stretched out like an anteater's tongue, sucking me into the unknown—a tropical broadleaf forest teeming with life. Down on the muddy ground, a smelly, boar-like peccary rooted in a log as a hairy tarantula crawled out. Up in the towering ceiba canopy, a black howler monkey screeched in the grip of some predator, then gurgled and ominously silenced. Everywhere in-between, ferns, vines, and orchids melded into a live, hanging tapestry, continually reweaving itself.

What response to this array of natural wonders could be appropriate? I performed an anticlimactic human trick; I turned a switch and surged forward.

Before my OJ ran dry, the capital city unfolded. While the rest of Belize is a hub for tourism and commerce, Belmopan is the hub of government worker activity. You guessed it: still as a tumbleweed ghost town. No greedy pirates here—several lawyers though. If you listen close, you can hear long departed bureaucrats shuffling papers back and forth for eternity. (Some folks think death is a termination. Others expect promotion or demotion. I'm thinking more lateral transfer.)

Jumping on the Hummingbird Highway, I rumbled across stone bridges and wound through banana plantations. One ripe, handy bunch caught my eye—a rare kind that tastes like buttered apples. Those small golden arches were the only fast food I'd pass that day. (On long, lonely drives, bananas also make great karaoke mics, but I wouldn't know about that.)

A slap-board trading post marked the intersection of an even-less-used road. I rolled to a stop. My truck's exhausted engine belched, sighed, and collapsed into a coma. The store stocked only two essential fuels: gas and beer. They had one type of petrol, two types of cerveza: Belikin Lager and Belikin Stout. Belize's national brew tastes great ice-cold in the jungle. Of course so does parrot piss. I mean it probably would.

The other high-octane liquid was the concern. My truck tank bore a sticker clearly reading "unleaded fuel only." I'm pretty good with tools. So I decided to attempt the necessary vehicle modifications. Climbing into the truck bed, I unbungee-corded a bin containing screwdrivers, wrenches, saws, and duct tape. Thirty minutes later, I was covered with mud, but the problem was solved: the sticker was completely scraped off.

Fully loaded and leaded, I chugged into Dangriga, my truck sounding like a constipated locomotive. Residents stared blankly as if to say, "I've seen stranger than you." The sleepy village straddles North Stann Creek, with Commerce Street crossing to become Saint Vincent, the isle from which the town founders migrated. The Garifuna inhabitants are a fun, chaotic people who excel in the arts but couldn't organize a cluster-fuck. Scotia bank was on the non-commerce side of the river—a bad omen.

I needed cash soon. Back in Canada, a Scotia manager swore my card would work at all branches. Yet in my heart I knew her freshly inked "Global Policies & Procedures Manual" didn't really envision some yahoo wandering around Southern Belize. I approached the ATM with unusual reverence and ceremony. I waited … no buckaroos. I cursed the faceless, heartless machine; I cursed the happy-faced, kind-hearted manager.

The bank was closed. Perhaps the malfunction was temporary; maybe everything would work another day. I crossed my fingers and pulled out onto the Southern Highway.

Civilization abruptly ended. The road line on my map was apparently someone's promise: "If you come, we will build it." Frequent signs proclaimed the route a United Nations/British Commonwealth/US Development Fund work-in-progress. I would've guessed more the joint efforts of me and a couple other passing trucks. Never say politicians do nothing but spend your money and take credit; they actually make some really nice signs.

Bedding down in the rainforest was an act of sheer brav—er—stupidity. Spider monkeys and fruit bats dangled above. Creepy-crawlies established supply lines over and under me. Passing cats left me to wonder: margay, ocelot, or jaguar? Don't even ask about the mosquitoes. By morning, I was as refreshed and relaxed as a heroin addict in detox. Just when I thought my hell was over, I made a discovery that may still send me into therapy: a crunchy, striped beetle in my navel. Save the rainforest? Save me from the rainforest! Try it yourself before you judge.

The final stretch to Punta Gorda was a journey into a lost world. Hordes of Mayan children peopled the landscape. Rivers served as highways, laundries, and public baths. Machetes worked as tools, weapons, and eating utensils.

Huts tripled as stores, kitchens, and chicken coops. Hammocks hosted naps, meals, and family reunions. Belize had transformed a Toyota Tundra into a time machine.

Rounding a bend, I came upon my destination. Punta Gorda's isolation stems from being at the end of the road—the not-yet-built road. Jungle-carpeted mountains and rugged, crashing coastline impede access to nearby Guatemala.

For centuries, this dead end kept the spot off the beaten track. While Native feet and Spanish boots traversed the Americas, this mist-shrouded, swampy nook was left to the chatter of birds and the smell of moss.

Today the continent's least-sought-after real estate sparkles as a scarce remnant of pristine biosphere, and seaside Punta Gorda attracts some who prefer life off of law enforcement's beaten track. One lazy afternoon, as the ocean clocked the centuries with its endless white-noise metronome, I showed up.

During my stay, most days ended at the Mangrove Restaurant. Jon, the Canadian owner who "moved south to avoid legal hassles," brings three assets to the fine-dining industry: he is handy with a baseball bat, he can/does out-drink the customers, and his wife makes steak, veggies, and garlic mashed potatoes more exciting than sex.

One night the place was packed. Missionary Larry and spouse sat at a corner table, under wall-mounted oars and fish netting. His income allowed for preaching the word, acquiring the primo Sea Front Inn, and building the area's only air-conditioned, high-rise condos with cable TV. Punta Gorda is a drug transshipment point; word-on-the-street puts the cleric at the epicenter. On a recent "fishing cruise," he was the sole survivor of a shipboard shootout.

Canoe and spears adorned the opposite wall, above Environmental Willy and family. Belizean born and Idaho educated, he returned home rich with endangered-species research grants. Alas, opening both a gym and a nightclub left him little time in the bush—except for the clear-cut section where he built his hurricane-proof mahogany-palace-on-stilts. He offered me work as his bartender. I can't mix drinks, but he figured I'd skim less profits than the local boys.

The room-center table held the mayor and his buxom fourth wife. They weren't drinking, because he was meeting-and-greeting, and she was thirteen.

Unexpectedly, a sinewy Rastafarian-type wearing tattered burlap and a yellow, crocheted cap, bounced in the door and plopped at my table. His voice sang out: "Hullo mon. Mi name iz Calico Jack. Haffa mi people wuz pirates, unna de Union Jack; de udda half sails below deck, cuz dem wuz black. Dats a fact!"

(Of those with their line polished to a rhyme, I usually stand clear, but I had the time, so I bought him a beer.) "What do you do Jack?"

"I wuz in de US Marine Corp, but dem kip tellinz mi wut ta do. So, I has ta get out. Now, I makes drums."

"What kind of drums?"

"De magic spirit drums!"

"Oh."

"Maybe ya cud loans me dat truck fer jus a little while."

When I declined, he produced a lab report with HIV POSITIVE circled. Leaning toward me, he threatened, "Sum udda folks iz fraid I might bite dem or sumptin, but you and meez good friends, right?"

Before I could respond, Jon came whipping round the bar with bat in furious motion. The rapscallion blew out like a gust of wind.

"I've told him not to pull that shit in here. Why don't you join us for a drink at the bar?"

I sat by a fiftyish American with military haircut and police manner. FBI Frank said he was buying drinks; actually, he was distributing truth serum. Drank most of it himself though; gave out more info than he gleaned. By the time he'd tried to buy my passport twice, I'd connected enough dots to know the grinning goof sitting next to him in Hawaiian shirt and flip-flops was a mafia snitch he was babysitting.

Lowering my voice, I suggested there was a fine line between prosecuting crime and manufacturing it, that I didn't appreciate being set up. Silence. His bloodshot, watery eyes smoldered with the knowledge his guise was transparent.

Regaining composure, he spoke: "Look kid, if I am what you say I am, and I'm not saying I am, you got no worries; you didn't take the bait. Let me give you some advice. Central America is not a touchy-feely place; everyone here has an angle. If you stay long enough, you'll be corrupted. I like you. Toughen up or go home!"

He was right. Long ago, the Spanish conquistadors imposed their ethic of power and gold on the indigenous cult of blood and fertility, until today the region is a macho, Darwinist stew, dominated by cash, guns, and push-up bras. Rich men buy power; poor men take power; women seduce power. Greed, pride, and lust, the basic instincts, the deadly sins, prevail.

Perhaps it is the same everywhere. Maybe, North American anti- monopoly, discrimination, and harassment laws simply coat our primal urges with a sophisticated veneer of political correctness, while the fire still burns down below.

Apparently, it has always been this way. In Christianity, greed of the eyes, lust of the flesh, and pride of life were the three temptations of Jesus. In Judaism as well as Islam the original forbidden fruit looked good to the eyes, tasted good to the flesh, and enhanced pride. Though ancient Ecclesiastes claims "there's nothing new under the sun"; current wisdom supposes a new evil in the world called terrorism. Belize, the pirate enclave, refreshed my memory that nothing could be further from the truth.

Like America today, Spain was once the global superpower. French, Dutch, and English new-world sailors were often hung as heretics, trespassers, and pirates. These underdogs felt modern terrorist sentiments, such as religious animosity ("infidel" galleons displayed the Catholic Virgin while English ships donned the Protestant Cross), economic exclusion (treasure convoys paraded the Caribbean declaring this private world trade center: "the Spanish Main"), and military disadvantage (Iberian conventional forces carried matchlock muskets and thrusting rapiers as seadogs bartered for weapons of mass destruction like fast flintlock guns and slashing cutlasses).

Spain constantly recruited European monarchs for a war-on-terrorism. Yet, this coalition of the almost willing was as steeped in conflict of interest as the Middle East is now. You see, the pirates were mostly state-sponsored terrorists.

For example, French-government-endorsed buccaneer Jean-David Nau tortured prisoners for fun. He burned them with matches, cut out their tongues, and once took a bite from a live captive's beating heart. This officially sanctioned psychopath was eventually dissected and possibly eaten by natives. (What wine does one serve with Frenchman?)

Dutch marauder Laurens de Graaf torched towns like Kuwaiti oil fields and raped like a war criminal before retiring to help pioneer Louisiana. (Hoodah madjin da great state uh Loozeeana hahbrin tehrists?)

When Englishman Francis Drake hijacked a Peruvian galleon during peacetime, Queen Bess affectionately named him "my pirate" and loaned him more ships. (Buckingham Palace's terrorism-tainted wealth has yet to be frozen by Parliament.)

After Britain seized Jamaica, Port Royal pirates were given authorization letters to wreck havoc on the enemy. Captain Henry Morgan stormed Porto Bello, Panama, using nuns and priests as human shields. At Maracaibo Bar,

Morgan foreshadowed September 11th by ramming a blazing commandeered vessel into a flagship.

One town defended itself with stampeding cattle. Morgan's raiders gunned the animals and tortured the people. (In fairness, the villagers did possess biological weapons: the cows. Not a civilian herd either, but elite bovine-guard combatants that littered the battlefield with squishy landmines.)

To placate Spain, England charged Morgan with piracy but never sentenced him. Rather, he was knighted, made deputy-governor of Jamaica, and buried in a church. Saddam never rewarded a terrorist more lavishly.

Will accountants cutting loose in yuppie bars someday replace Captain Morgan's Spicy Rum with Wacky Osama Bin Lager? Hopefully not. Yet, history suggests that yesterday's terrorist is tomorrow's naughty nave. Even in his lifetime, Morgan was jointly dubbed "defender of Jamaica" and "terror of the Spanish Main." Kind of depends which end of the blunderbuss you're on.

Of course most of this was white-on-brown terror. Since the world's brown people are continually surrounded by terror, they find it less terrifying; therefore, it isn't really terrorism—something like that. Actually, terrorism is no newcomer to Northern latitudes either.

Does US Homeland Security know that in 1696, the New England surveyor-general called Rhode Island "the chief refuge for pirates"? Or that in 1717, the colonial secretary of Pennsylvania estimated 1,500 pirate ships stalked the coast? Or that New York Governor Fletcher befriended pirate Thomas Tew, who hijacked Islamic shipping? Or that North Carolina Governor Eden took a cut of Blackbeard's loot and performed his wedding? Or that, long before guys named Mohammed used fake ID to bypass airport boarding gates, America was born of the Boston Tea Piracy, wherein "anti-government extremists" used Native garb to bypass ship-port boarding planks and tea bomb the harbor, thus sabotaging trade (for you conservatives), and dumping in wetlands (for you liberals), just to make a political statement?

Does the UN Security Council know that in 1776, the Continental Congress authorized piratical looting of British civilian craft, inspiring the French Convention to go even further, urging corsairs to board English ships with axes and "cut down those proud islanders, despots of the ocean"? Or that Benjamin Franklin sponsored hostage-taking forays for swapping with American prisoners, and then John Paul Jones was awarded a congressional medal for carrying them out?

Does the Pentagon remember enlisting and pardoning pirate Jean Lafitte, who Andrew Jackson called "hellish banditti"? Or refusing, along with Spain and others with weak conventional navies, to sign the 1856 Paris Declaration, outlawing privateer-style terrorism?

Throughout history, those with conventional weapons licked their enemies with conventional war. Sometimes because of scruples, mostly for the same reason dogs lick themselves: because they can. Those warriors who couldn't often broke the rules, because while "most men lead lives of quiet desperation," some believe "desperate times call for desperate measures."

When golden-age piracy ceased serving the needs of Western states and increasingly threatened the merchant community, navy actions and hangings commenced in earnest. Historically, terrorism was the enemy of commerce, not law and order. The most successful pirate—Black Bart Roberts—didn't drink, forbade gambling, and prescribed shipboard Bible reading. Yet, agents of the Common*wealth* hung his crew.

First Century Roman historian Dio Cassius said, "There was never a time when piracy was not practiced. Nor may it cease to be as long as the nature of mankind remains the same." Ancient Persians blockaded the Tigris against pirates. Greeks of the Iliad feared piratical attacks. Romans posted anti-piracy patrols. Arab traders skirted piracy-prone shores. Spanish settlers loathed piratical Euro-trash. English merchants cursed colonists who hid, supported, and acquitted pirates. Today, America wears the target that traditionally emblazons the official-global-superpower T-shirt.

Whether you side with Western democracies (and the godless anarchy of shopping malls at Christmas), or Eastern regimes (and the old-world charm of Lorena-Bobbit-style jurisprudence), there is no war-on-terrorism (or on infidels), unless you believe propaganda is what your enemy does, but publicity is what you do.

What we have here is the ongoing clash of cultures and civilizations. Underdogs still fight underhandedly. England, Spain, and America still hang pirates highhandedly. France still skulks in old haunts, uncertain whether to ambush dangerous Moors or sanctimonious Yankees. Turkey still wavers between East and West. (Just as Americans felt uncomfortable with Janet Reno wacking the wackos from Waco [since kooky Koresh and company were citizens], many Easterners feel proprietary concern for their in-house nut mix.)

Back when racism was fashionable, you could identify the teams by their colors. The lunatic-fringe jihad could be called badass Bedouins, falafel-eating Huns, or Barbarians at the boarding gate. Thankfully, current Western society strives to embrace good people of all skin tones. So we are burdened with the nebulous scare-word: terrorism, which—depending on the century—fits any of the historical players.

Don't expect national leaders to clear up the confusion; politicians get extra points for attacking evils abroad. Osama stood up to "the infidels"; Bush stood up to "the terrorists"; Chretien stood up to "the bastards" (as Member of Canadian Parliament Carolyn Parrish referred to Americans). All got a popularity boost. Conversely, moralizing to one's own culture is hazardous. Ghandi lectured Hindus and Muslims;

Jesus lectured Jews; Martin Luther King lectured Christians. Everyone got killed.

One of these failed motivational speakers said, "Take the log out of your own eye, before removing the speck in your neighbor's." Why?

Speck visibility is no problem. Ask most Westerners about cultures that pursue politics by strapping on bombs then jumping on buses; you'll instantly feel the moral outrage. Ask most Easterners about societies that pursue fulfillment by taking parents to retirement homes, spouses to divorce court, children to daycare, and pregnancies to abortion clinics; you'll sense an equally clear vision. (Simply paralleling these worldviews may relegate my writing to Polynesia, legendary literary tolerance notwithstanding.)

Surgically-accurate speck-removal is no challenge either. A surgical strike on an Eastern nation is much easier than, say, getting a Western pilot's union to forego hot food and flirtation for locking the cockpit door. Likewise, any Mid-East mob knows burning an American flag is much simpler than duplicating American prosperity.

Possibly, "Take the log out of your own eye, before removing the speck in your neighbor's" means that focusing foremost on others' sins is hypocritical. Westerners can easily dodge this censure from an Eastern rabbi with our culture's greatest weapon: the legal technicality. After all, no one who saw the September 11th footage would dare call it a speck, and anyone who recalls history knows that terrorism isn't in our neighbor's eye. Terrorism is in the eye of the beholder.

Appropriately, my return from Belize was hindered more by gringo eye logs than foreign rascals. At home, spilling boiled water on my foot would be no big deal. However, in the tropics, it festered into a green-pus-oozing infection. (Rum is healthier than oatmeal for breakfast!) A sadistic, tweezers-wielding nurse saved my foot, mercilessly swabbing alcohol-drenched gauze, while I cried for my mommy.

Phoning the Scotia Bank president saved my gluteus maximus as well. I explained that without immediate funds I'd have neither transportation nor food. In short, I'd be in the situation most brown people face everyday. Naturally, he was terrified and arranged the transfer.

My last Belizean memory comes from the white beaches of Placencia Peninsula. Anglers reeled in fighting bonefish and big barracuda as swimmers touched velvety stingrays and sandpapery sharks.

Burying my toes in warm sand, I watched a diving group bound for Glover's Reef, named after a buccaneer. Their guide explained that pirates once inhabited Belize. Bullshit! They still do.

I don't expect any kudos from luxury tour operators or retirement villa brokers for saying that. Yet, for every boy who dreams of being a pirate and every man who dreams of being a boy, for every girl who prefers SUVs to minivans and every women who doesn't relish the government databasing her shopping purchases with bank records, DNA, and retina scan, it's good to know there are still places where you make your own rules, where no one tells you to take your feet off the furniture.

Belize is such a place. Even the swaying coconut palms betray a pirate's heart, whispering that the blue caribe offers all you could ever want or need—except a job.

The Globalization Grinch Who Sponsored Christmas

Guatemala doesn't need its infamous roving guerrilla bands to be dangerous. As I stood at the port of entry, throngs of peasants walked around or through the checkpoint without presenting identification. Officials appeared not to notice and devoted their time to the monied foreigners. Since the country's frontiers often consist of tiny shallow rivers in unpatrolled jungles, it's probably a safe bet that anyone respecting law enough to cross at a border station means no harm.

Inside my first night's hotel room, a bulky television set tilted semi-securely on an overhead wall bracket—that is, as long as no one accidentally opened the door too far. In such a case, the careless soul would instantly be snatched from the gene pool by natural selection. If one avoided death-by-Sony, the ceiling fan wobbled like a fat kid with a hoola-hoop at approximately gringo eye-level. If one bypassed the whirling cornea-transplant, the shower offered a water-heating device consisting of an on/off switch attached to tangled wires wrapped around the showerhead with exposed live ends dangling inches from the water flow. After surviving this mid-range Guatemalan hotel, it seemed only fair to me that those living in safe little hovels should have to contend with execution squads.

I'd entered the country through Mexico's Soconusco Valley, by the same route Spanish conquistador Pedro de Alvarado used in 1523. However, this time the indigenous people were ready. The local Sunday market offered the usual non-touristy things: vegetables, fruits, grains, live chickens, dead chickens, disassembled chickens, blankets, spices, firewood, coffee, chocolate, soap, rope, boots, cowboy hats, guns, machetes, baskets, pots, candles, crucifixes, knock-off clothes, and rip-off CDs, but it also sported a plethora of genuine Mayan souvenir mugs, key chains, and baseball caps. Some bore a mysterious faded hieroglyphic vaguely resembling the words: "Made in the People's Republic of China."

I took a pass on the trinkets and hopped a bus. The smell of bananas, papaya, coconut, and pineapple and the sound of birds, insects, children, and marimba faded away as we ascended from the sweltering coastal rainforest into the cool mountain pines. We eventually leveled-off then began a ferocious serpentine descent. When the driver had initially told me how few quetzals I needed to pay for the ride, I figured someone had made a mistake. Someone had. That would be me. This was not the rich-and-demanding-tourist bus; this was the poor-and-ready-to-meet-Jesus-campesino bus. If you struggle to lift your thoughts from the worldly to the eternal, I highly recommend this form of transport.

Brakes squealed, babies squalled, luggage flew, and rubber burned. Though the rusty Blue Bird school bus had been retired from US service decades ago for safety reasons, it now rattled and flung around blind hairpin turns with horrifying centrifugal force. Passengers braced limbs and grabbed strangers to avoid becoming projectiles. Behind schedule and accustomed to navigating by faith not sight, our pilot swerved and dodged oncoming trucks, cars, motorcycles, bicycles, toddlers, and goats. My face turned white then green. Only one thing kept me from screaming to be let off: the presence of the old woman behind me, vice-gripping her grandson, fingering her rosary, and staring stoically ahead as she did every day of her life.

We arrived in Antigua stunned and starved. No welcome could've been better than the relaxing sound of Fidel Funes' Orchestra and the candlelit sight of our traditional Mayan feast. We sampled kak-ik (spicy orange turkey stew), sopa tortuga (savory-herbed turtle soup), pepian de pollo (chicken with chayote/pumpkin dressing), gallo en chicha (rooster with sweet red woody sauce), tepezcuintle (grilled fox/dog/weasel-like mammal), pupusas (fat cheesy tortillas with radish salad), and a banana leaf tamal. Washed it all down with the smooth black Guatemalan beer Moza and slept for ten hours.

Woke up to streaming sunshine and a whim to tour a coffee plantation. The day was gorgeous, but the java estate was disappointing. In the greenhouse, we watched drudging assembly-line workers scotch-taping Arabica stems onto Robusta roots, for plants that could survive the current drought and still be marketed as 100% Arabica. Legal but unromantic. I didn't think Juan Valdez would approve.

We next viewed the opulent stables where the proprietor kept his pedigreed horses, and the slightly inferior accommodations where the women harvesters lived. Our guide boasted of the owner's generosity in building this dormitory "so the children could be with their mothers."

"Do the kids work too?" someone sheepishly asked.

Mister Public Relations cleared his throat, "Why, yes. It's wonderful. The adults can reach the high beans and the children pick the low ones."

How perfect, I thought, fuckin' Shangri-La!

Time to take a break from humanity and climb an active volcano. Though I no longer felt much like a virgin, perhaps I would throw myself in. Not that a modern person would seek to appease the angry gods—I just wanted to shut out their voices.

Mount Pacaya, like my libido, has been continuously active for decades. As we strode up the burro-dropping-and-volcanic-rock-strewn trail through lush forest, my guide remained continuously silent behind his Ray Bans. I chose him solely for his name: Emmanuel, which means "God with us." I'm not usually superstitious, but I don't usually walk across hot lava either. (Hmmm, God with us, guiding us across hot lava—sounds like an old Tony Robbins seminar.)

Above the timberline, we trekked over charcoal-gray extinct lava and ash-white avalanche debris. The panorama stretched from golden-cloud-covered Pacific Ocean below to glowing-red-veined black summit above—heaven and hell flipped over. Suddenly, I felt and smelt something amiss. Just as many religious folks had predicted, my sole was burning. They were new boots, too. I hustled on up the moonscape, past lava flows so thick they appeared motionless.

The ground became ever more treacherous: up then down, cold and razor sharp then hot and melting away beneath your feet. Finally, I reached a rushing near-blinding River Styx, into which I thrust my walking pole to see it burst into flame and move steadily down the stream, like an Olympic torch for the Hadean games. A bit dramatic? It is, because it was. Hiked down the mountain and caught a van ride to Lago Atitlan.

On the shore of this crater lake—deep as an abyss, framed by volcanoes high as the heavens—lies the hippie town and transport center of Panajachel. On the patio of the Sunset Café, drinking Cerveza Cabro, listening to Gypsy Kings Flamenco, and gazing at the reflective water extending from the embarcadero, lay I.

The truth is I like hippies, but after a couple brews, I uninhibitedly asked one, "If all you need is love, why do you guys tote around such wacky ideas?" No longer welcome at the café, I caught a gently-rocking boat for the Tz'utujil Mayan capital of Santiago Atitlan. Some tourists from Philadelphia bitched about our slow passage while the fresh breeze and idyllic view made me wish the small sputtering engine would conk out altogether.

We docked in the midst of a purple-and-green-clad indigenous crowd. Women sported vibrant woven skirts; men donned cowboy hats and cotton shorts. A shaman held the older gents spellbound by lewdly demonstrating the benefits of a medicinal herb for prostate trouble. The hunched and wrinkled group howled and clucked with laughter.

I hailed a red golf-cart-like taxi called a tuc-tuc and drove to the current shrine of the ancient deity Maximom. "The mam" resides in a different house each year and (if not sleeping) accepts visitors offering cash, cigars, or booze. He's sort of a bully god who grants prayers for greed or revenge.

Most locals don't take Maximom too seriously. Like the town's rapidly-growing charismatic church, he offers a way to extend the middle finger to the historically force-fed Catholicism, which many perceive as the ally of their rich oppressors.

The shrine guardians and I shared some laughs followed by some swigs of Quetzalteca. This raw-cane-spirit Mayan moonshine can make you see visions or go blind. Groping for the door, I bumped into the sacred figurine and apologized profusely.

The caretakers said, "He appreciates apologies but prefers money."

I said, "Who doesn't?"

They said, "Good point."

I said, "Goodbye." Of all the deities I've offended, the wrath of Maximom weighs least heavy on my mind.

Heading back through the fruit market, I made friends and requested photos. Many Maya feel uncomfortable being photographed and have a vague mystical sense that such snapshots take a piece of their souls. Others have a very concrete practical sense that such pictures should be highly compensated.

One lady expressed glee at my photo suggestion but insisted I must buy three of the dresses she held. I said they were beautiful but that (unlike many other men from California) I don't wear dresses. She responded (roughly translated), "It's not about you, you idiot, it's so my kids can go to school!" A truer word was never spoken, but perhaps the refreshing charm of honesty in business has its limits.

On the return boat, I sat by Amelia. This newly-wealthy Mayan businesswoman was going on vacation. She exuded excitement over her premier opportunity to be on the tourist side of the camera. I watched when she set her first foot down on the other side of the lake then looked around like Christopher Columbus. There will always be new worlds as long as there are new eyes.

My last Guatemalan memory comes from the village of Malacatan. I detoured there to see the annual Christmas tree inauguration, which I expected to be a heartwarming folksy affair. No such luck. Around the town square, towering state-of-the-art amplifiers blared out a thumping backbeat. This would be the least shocking of many surprises.

The impoverished municipality had apparently traded the magic of Christmas for the financial wizardry of corporate sponsorship. The plaza was framed with lush Ceiba trees once held sacred by the Maya but today used to hang inflatable bottles of Gallo, the salty pale-yellow beer of Guatemala since 1896. Not tacky enough? Atop the soaring, glittering, twinkling pine tree sat the Gallo rooster logo.

Near the central gazebo waited a portable bandstand and an unattended artillery barrage of open-mouthed firework cannons. A flimsy encircling string sought to discourage the numerous children from playing with the explosives. Only a few did. Most were otherwise occupied stomping in the gasoline puddles flowing from the petroleum station next door. (While Darwin's travels confirmed his belief in survival of the fittest, mine have only postulated survival of the damn lucky.)

My attentive concern was short-lived. Suddenly, the bandstand lit up like a Vegas show, the music convulsed into electronic pop, and out danced the Gallo Girls in red & black Sporty Spice outfits with blinding cubic zirconium in their tight navels. My shameless slack jaw could only mouth the words: "God bless Guatemala."

I enjoyed being the tallest guy in the crowd and hearing my favorite songs, even with the word Gallo strangely inserted throughout the lyrics. I might've even supported a yuletide pitch to drink the national beer, if 90% of the audience hadn't been twelve years old.

Of course, these were the same Mayan preteens who drove their newborn babies around town on ATVs. Maybe they were ready for other mature decisions, like which brand of beer would form part of their lifetime identity. Perhaps the born-in-a-manger stuff would only confuse, since this qualifies as luxury accommodations in Guatemala. And of all the foreign deities imposed on the Maya, which has brought more joy to this corner of the world than beer? My motto: If you can't lick 'em, drink 'em. Can't seem to find any notes from the rest of the evening.

Doubtless many readers will share my chagrin to see this classic culture absorbed into the globalization machine. And as for those who consider globalization a unique opportunity to employ children or sell them garbage, may they rot in hell. Still, as long as people travel, trade, and innovate, the world will continue shrinking. The Maya may even have begun the process that now threatens to engulf them. Their awe-inspiring pyramids were as much centers of commerce as spirituality; their ancient entrepreneurs, who gathered to swap cocoa beans and seashells, were as eager for multi-national expansion as anyone listed on today's New York Stock Exchange.

Like it or not, all cultures are forever changing and forever changed. Such is life on earth. Perhaps we love to climb mountains because they seem so eternal, while everything else appears so transitory. Yet, volcanic eruptions shatter the illusion of permanence, spewing forth new earth even as the old is tucked underground along deep-sea portals, destined for the fiery subterranean melting pot into which the minerals comprising both mountains and our bodies will eventually be folded. So, climb those lofty peaks and visit those nostalgic peoples while you can, because they do symbolize the only eternal reality, which is change.

Liberty, Equality

& Fries with Gravy

Flying into Montreal, you pass over rippling forests and myriad lakes resembling a green carpet often snagged and peed on by a bad puppy. Next come Lego-brick suburbs, the mighty Saint Lawrence River, and bonjour Pierre Elliot Trudeau airport. Outside the terminal, faces are happier and arms are hairier than in British Canada. I take a taxi downtown.

Blue-oxidized church spires stab above the gray stone cityscape, as does a fifty-foot La SENZA bra model. Reddish-brunette lovelies sporting mirrored sunglasses, white stretch undershirts, and designer jeans abound. At one intersection, a towering video screen shows nude women cavorting over text advertising "contact dance." A local news exposé found this typically means that shapely girls from Latin America rub against the pockets of homely men from North America to make contact with the appendage and coinage that reside there. Close encounters of the third-world-migrant-exploitive kind.

Exit the cab at Fairmount Bakery. In this Jewish neighborhood alley, the Shlafman family has been hand-rolling and wood-firing Montreal's first and most renowned bagel since 1919. I squeeze in between ceiling-high racks to speak to a counter girl with kinky flour-dusted hair. "Two poppy seed please." The crisp grainy shell and soft warm center leave me as eager to exploit the city as Duddy Kravitz.

I set out walking through the heart of this metropolis that long ago embraced the chic. Here director Denys Arcand once defined the cultural edge with his films "Jésus of Montreal" and "Le Déclin de l´ Empire Américain." Here I stroll past dark empty gothic basilicas and packed trendy fashion boutiques. Even my stride must bow to fad. Fellow pedestrians don't pause for crossing signals like English Canadians but traverse the street whenever the crowd does. (Local custom dictates you should always be dressed to stop traffic anyway.)

It seems there's a smugness to Montreal hip. Even the twenty year olds profess to appreciate black-American jazz and Quebec-government-funded documentaries about white-American racism. Yet, do these fashionistas realize that the Southern slave system was not so much abolished as expanded to include them, that the textile plantation big house now extends from the Rio Grande to the Arctic Sea, that beyond our privileged borders—shackled by barriers to free competition—the global masses sweat and toil to keep our teenagers sweet and spoiled with the style of the moment? As Elizabeth Hurley says, "You can't have fashion without victims."

Newsflash: Mississippi is no longer the center of the cotton or exploitation universe. Yet upstanding North Americans still organize to protect their standard of living from the "undesirables." Don't bash the Klan if you oppose free trade. Labor unions that beg (or bribe) politicians to exclude them from the jungle of global commerce might as well ask four swarthy Negroes to carry them on a bamboo platform over the unpleasantness of a literal rainforest.

Shame on you unswarthy metrosexual Obama for pandering to the rust belt, promising to oppose trade agreements, and supporting the Jim Crow separation that keeps our Latin American friends down or sneaking across the border to learn contact dance. Are they not men and brothers? Or ... um ... really sexy sisters? The white sheets of paper on which auto-workers petition against free commerce are not so unlike the white sheets that Mississippians donned in times past, born of fearful desperation to halt privilege from slipping away. The world is not a just place, but woe to those who seek to bolster the injustice.

Detroit, oh Detroit, how often has the federal government taken you under its wing when it should've forced you to be competitive? But you were not willing. Michigan, oh Michigan, how bravely we Yankees fought against misguided confederates who clung to prosperity built on the backs of others! Now, it is your economy that needs reconstruction, your confederations that won't let us imagine a Lennonist-but-not-Leninist brotherhood of man. Why not embrace free commerce just because it's right, without waiting for "trampling out of the vintage where the grapes of wrath are stored"?

Perverting Neil Young, Northern man, I've seen your employee syndicates claiming to protect the little guy while actually defending the middle-America guy against the little foreign guy. Best remember what your good book manifesto says: "Solidarity now, workers of the world unite!" If slave-holding, brown-sugar-contact-dancing Thomas Jefferson could intellectually grasp that all men are created equal, maybe pension-holding, sweeten-my-contract-demanding union bosses could do the same.

Isn't it time the sweaty darkies were allowed into the big house for a long overdue glass of lemonade? It's true that Scarlett O'Hara may lose space for clothes, since globalization tends to equalize. However, the world didn't end in the last millennium, though brown people were starving; it probably won't end in the next, even if some North Americans have to walk to work. Globalization ushers in a frightening new world. Yet, no moral person can oppose it, any more than he could've opposed the emancipation proclamation for making him compete with cheap-labor freedmen.

Feeling like a modern abolitionist, I strut a little too self-righteously past Uncle Tom Hilfiger's storefront and out of the designer clothing district. By midnight, I sit in La Belle Province on Rue Sainte Catherine. Vinyl booths, neon lights, chrome chairs, and flashing gumball machines surround me. The aroma of poutine—zingy beef gravy over fries with cheese curds—wafts up at me from my plate. Yummy, cheap, and filling.

The gritty, nostalgic, 24-hour diner's artery-clogging special recalls to me the title of Kathy Reichs' Montreal crime mystery *Death Du Jour*. (Yes, the book the TV series "Bones" was based on. [Yes, the show with the forensic anthropologist babe. Can I finish my story now?]) Poutine is not just tasty junk food; it's the only method of assisted suicide legal in Catholic Quebec. While pre-mortem gravy stains aren't exactly dying with dignity, it's still a delicious and rebellious way to go. I gorge myself proudly as a protest against nanny government seeking to protect my job or my health by crushing global human freedom. Let the cry go forth from this (late) time and (hip) place: "Vive la liberté, égalité, et fries avec gravy!"

Politicos, Priests & Pedophiles

John's boy-toy lit a smoke. The cigarette wasn't the only thing smoldering that morning. As the young Mexican struck a pose on the blue silk couch, John sashayed in, wearing too little clothing and too much cologne. Old gringo knees peeked out from under his kimono; a bald spot shone through wet, combed-over hair.

"Did everyone meet my friend?" John sang out. "Oscar showed up last night and slept in my room—on the floor." No one had asked. The guests staying in his apartment had other concerns: breakfast was laden with dead ants, there was no drinkable water, plus the air was sweltering hot and rank with dog urine.

The heat was normal. Tapachula is a steamy border town a few miles from Guatemala. Translucent geckos hung motionless on the wall, while sticky papaya and mango trees breathed just outside the window. Sweat clustered on upper lips and lower backs.

Ants were also typical. In a fertile rainforest where typhoid and salmonella are frequent dining companions, mere bugs were as usual and ignored as plate-side parsley garnish. But the plagues of drought and stench had less routine causes.

The previous Monday, John decided he wanted a puppy. Enter Rusty—yipping, biting ankles, falling over from the weight of his ears. On Tuesday, John decided to visit Spain. The unhousebroken hound was left solo to explore and redecorate his new home.

John returned Sunday to host traveling norteamericanos. Marching us upstairs to our accommodations, he unlocked the condo/kennel and waved us in. Our eyes began to water.

"Oh Rusty, I forgot about youuuuu!" John squealed. Kissing the dog on the lips, he penitently poured bottled, purified water into multiple doggie bowls. John's other pet, Oscar, arrived that night and washed his hair with the rest. Next day, we awoke to discover our place in the circle of life.

The weirdness only got weirder. My wanderings in Chiapas became a journey into the dark realms of sexual, political, and even metaphysical child abuse.

John owned a posh English school for kids. Entering the facility one day, I was blasted with the sound of the Village People and enough air-conditioning to give a guy perky nipples. "You can get yourself clean; you can have a good meal; you can do whatever you feel; it's fun to stay at the Y-M-C-A ..." John stopped the music. A floor-sprawled group of small brown faces stared angelically up at him. Explaining the concept of communal showers, he had them stand and mimic washing each other. John began psuedo-scrubbing his own body parts. Too many parts.

Afterward, I stood by stunned. "Have you seen my new van?" John broadcast across the room, pointing me to a shiny behemoth parked outside. "I'm setting up a charity foundation with our local orphans' home. On weekends the children can ride to my beach house and swim in the pool."

"Oh, goody," I mumbled.

A naïve-seeming Australian missionary wearing a calla-lily-print dress greeted me at "the orphans' home." I had come during siesta. Precious, dirty munchkins dreamed away on wafer-thin mats on marble floor. The crumbling villa held no furniture or diversions ... except a swimming pool. Why would anyone buy a van to drive the kids an hour away to another one? I asked her why the government placed those children there. "Most were sexually abused," she said. "The little blokes are very vulnerable."

John's beach-house party began at sunset. Next to his Greco-Roman pool stood a palapa (palm-frond-covered gazebo), where hard-drinking patrons lounged in wobbly hammocks. Our inebriated host bellowed "Hellooooo!" to all newcomers, then furrowed his brow in a futile attempt to recognize them. A buffet table offered a choice of rum and coke, rum and tequila, rum and rum, or guacamole. "Chips might be coming later."

After all bottles had been emptied, broken, or misplaced, the fiesta migrated to the surf. John gathered up his employees, "Okay, everybody take off your shirts and let's do a Bay Watch photo." (In Mexico, business underlings have few rights; the only time I heard the word "harass" in a corporate context, it turned out to be two words.) Human-pyramid pics followed bouncing-across-the-beach shots. Then came the magical mystery tour of John's house.

Guestrooms for sleepovers made up the ground floor; a master suite filled out the top story. This lofty perch could only be accessed by a precarious, retractable ladder reminiscent of childhood bunk beds. John's bedroom included a big screen TV with a disturbing mix of Disney and adult videos. Beyond a group-sized Jacuzzi, workers were constructing a false end-wall to conceal a cramped, windowless chamber. "What's it for?" I asked.

John replied, "Ummmmm … well … I, uh, haven't decided yet."

Señor Tovar was Mexican consulate to Guatemala. The smiling, portly diplomat sat on a Ralph Lauren, riveted-leather sofa by a bookshelf displaying Twain, Hemingway, Cervantes, a University of Utah diploma, and a PC with Britney Spears screensaver. We drank black coffee under sluggishly orbiting fans. "The Mexico/Guatemala frontier has a seedy history," he sighed. "Northbound Central Americans swim the river. Children arrive penniless, desperate … totally exploitable."

Señor Coutier had a thin, red moustache and the largest hacienda in the valley. "You want to know about prostitution, no?"
"Yes."
"Well, I own this town. Ask anybody."
"Yes."
"You can buy a child's innocence for a hundred pesos. If I were a pervert, I would live here." He hoisted his shot glass. "I am a Frenchman by blood and a Mexican by birth and I hate all gringos."
"There are no French men. Only French women."
"Su Madre" (screw your mother).
"Let's make peace and drink …" (we cautiously raised our glasses as I changed my mind) "to your sister." The rest of this enlightened exchange I cannot recall.

An ultra-light airplane is what they call it. Looks more like a kite and a lawnmower had a lovechild. By the time the teeth-rattling gadget reached take-off speed, I deeply regretted my thrill-seeking death wish. Alas, the bumpy stubble runway, hacked out of a cornfield, had come to an end. No choice but to fly.
Antonio, the pilot, refused to accept that I couldn't hear over winds that stretched my face and bent my nose. He babbled non-stop as I nodded uncomprehendingly. Whenever he paused for a response, I blurted out, "Si!"
Fear transformed into awe, which metamorphed into the experience of a lifetime. Below us, ash-wisping peaks belted the arc of the planet. Vast, lush plantations alchemied sunlight into fruit. Oceanic zirconium shimmered and melded seamlessly into sky.

Dropping into a glide, our flimsy shadow traced sandy beaches and white surf. Barnstorming a pasture, our buzz-by evoked unknowable conversation between expressionless Brahma bulls. Peasant farmers waved straw hats at the heaven-sent miracle-machine I so recently disparaged.

From an eagle's perspective the world was so beautiful. Mossy lagoons looked idyllic; crowded schoolyards looked happy, because from up there you could see neither mosquitoes nor any other creatures that prey on human flesh.

San Cristobal was a couple hundred miles and a couple hundred years from Tapachula. Highway wound through pine forest and mountain air grew cold as I exchanged my *oscillating fan*tasies for *wood-burning stove pipe*dreams. Tzotzil Mayans stared at me with wind-chiseled stone faces. These indigenous soil-tillers laboriously coaxed corn and chilies from dizzying alpine ledges where I'd fear to tread.

8:52 a.m. 2100 meters. Crested a peak. The morning sun fire-flashed from under the horizon in a blinding ambush. Braking reflexively, my hands shot up a blockade. White light rushed through thin air and pierced the steeple of my outstretched arms. Squinting eyes refocused. Nestled in the summit crater before me were the glistening red roofs of the colonial town.

Stopped at Casa del Pan for breakfast.

"Buenos dias, señor."

"Buenos dias. Quiero huevos a la mexicana y tortillas, jugo naranja y cafe con leche."

"Bueno."

"Gracias."

A mural, brush stroked across the back wall, called out for attention. On the left were Commandante Marcos and his masked Zapatista rebels, who commandeered the city in January 1994; on the right were the army soldiers who drove them back into the jungle—revolution verses the system. Larger scale and centered was an indigenous woman with baby and breast. (I'm not saying I noticed things in that order.) If the hippie-owned vegetarian eatery was a Bohemian church serving daily mass of tofu and chai, then the Mayan Madonna was perfectly enshrined: maternal innocence tormented by warring demons steeped in the original sin of testosterone. I decided to fight the power; I'd find a steak place for dinner.

Drove to the crowded plaza, parked and walked. I felt like Jesus or The Rolling Stones. Flesh pressed against me from all sides, grabbing, groping. Wrinkled faces, wounded faces, hungry faces, all pleaded for my blessing. What miracle had I performed for such celebrity status? I'd driven a late-model vehicle into an impoverished community. Suddenly, a small wad of pesos and dollars seemed like a tumor within me. I extended smiles and warmth more to receive grace than give it.

The square hummed with jittery anticipation of something yet undefined. Truckloads of Tzotziles and Tzeltales arrived sporadically from the countryside to mull around in silence. The usual tourist hordes dwindled to a sprinkling of hapless students as government sentries nervously shuffled, tightening their gun grips. Vendors packed away colorful, meticulously woven huipiles while buyers snatched up crudely crafted Zapatista dolls.

Darkness fell. Each moment, fewer faces and more faceless masks surrounded me. By donning scraps of black wool, individuals submerged themselves into the anonymous mob. Saw one other white guy. I was keenly aware of standing on the very spot where light-skinned Catholics once "punished" dark skins who wouldn't convert.

Around me, infants sweated and squalled behind their masks. Would the coveted political liberation compensate for their discomfort? Sadly, children can be exploited ideologically as well as sexually.

Surfing the crowd, I heard gossip on what the movement would bring: land redistribution/land communalization, economic progress/traditional commerce, political representation/political independence. Like most charismatic leaders, Marcos apparently fanned widespread hopes into flames, seldom extinguishing them with any well-defined agenda.

El Commandante arrived. Honking trucks circled the zocalo with chanting riders waving machetes. The balaclava-clad hero emerged from an arterial side street flanked by strutting compadres. Wind gusted. Chanting amplified. I stuck out my hand in an apolitical gesture carrying no loftier motive than capturing an I-was-there moment. He shook it. I went back to my hotel. He led a march to Mexico City.

I glided down the open road under a baby-blue sky, in a shiny, white truck spattered with terra-cotta mud. You could almost smell the freedom. Condors soared effortlessly over the endless ocean of palms and volcanoes.

I slowed down for a family of iguanas sprawled on the pavement. My wheels grinded to a halt as the greeny-gray dinosaurs shuffled grudgingly off their asphalt sun-spa. I stopped the engine to listen to the silence. Soon bird music wafted across the highway through the passenger window; parrots and macaws clustered on roadside trees. Where was I going in such a hurry?

I took a detour to Agua Azul. The famous natural wonder was barricaded behind row upon row of recreational vehicles—the retirement version of Woodstock. Nevertheless, the phenomenon was breathtaking. Cascading through the rainforest was the bluest water I'd ever seen, like neon, turquoise Perrier, bubbling and giggling from pool to pool. Nature so perfect it looked unnatural.

Instantly, paradise was lost. A thundering herd of the saggiest, droopiest tourists wearing the least allowed by law splashed across my line of sight. Buying a sangria-flavored soda, I sat down under a thatched cabana. My mind reflected on a pristine world invaded by humanity's imperfections. Wilderness, like children, can be violated.

At the next table sat a group of Mexican women glaring contemptuously at a group of Mexican men, who stared obliviously at a television—The Three Stooges. Though comprehending no dialogue, the beer-laden hombres howled with laughter. I, too, became entranced by the screen, losing myself in the universal charm of grown men hitting each other with sharp tools.

Next day, I visited the jungle-overgrown pyramids of Palenque. Viewed from the surrounding hills, the stone pinnacles poke through the forest canopy like islands in a vast, green sea. The monuments testify to the specific genius of the Mayans, as well as the general impudence of humans. These man-made mountains originally outglitzed Mother Nature's version. But Mom always has the last word. While the Sierra Madre erode gracefully into hills, Palenque crumbles rapidly into ruins.

My feet padded softly across a grassy clearing abandoned by barefoot warriors a thousand years before. A watchful presence remained. Spirits could be felt on the edge of the forest like elusive jaguars. Toucans and howler monkeys chattered.

Beyond the Temple of the Inscriptions and the Tomb of Pakal the Great loomed the Palace Complex. I panted up the massive steps. Giant rodents scurried all around the granite ghost town.

Stone relief portrayed enemies captured, tortured, and sacrificed. Hearts were gouged out. Swollen genitals were mutilated. Priestly-garbed executioners axed young victims in the Americas' longest-running action flick.

Warning barriers marking the four-story central tower off-limits had been knocked facedown. I ascended unawares. The apex offered a 360-degree panorama and a rock-slab altar—a mystical, bloodstained place. Anguished last gasps still seemed to hover on the wind.

I wondered how many lives had been ceremonially snuffed on that spot. The human longing for immortality has always empowered religion for good and evil. As pedophiles exploit our hunger to be loved and politicos exploit our hunger to be free, so priests exploit our hunger just to be.

"But Palenque was pagan religion," some would say. "Catholic priests hadn't yet reached the new world." True. They were busy sacrificing innocents in crusades for Jerusalem—the mystical, bloodstained site of the old world. "But those were primitive times," the objection goes on. "Religions don't sacrifice children today."

I had visions of Latin America's prepubescent masses, begging, oozing infection, shining shoes, bagging other people's tasty-looking groceries for twelve-hour shifts: bright-eyed kids: children birthed in unsustainable numbers: toddlers who must cross highways without supervision because parents must have sex without contraception. Why? Because religion demands it—coitus Vaticanus.

The origin of this ongoing ritual is as old and pagan as Palenque. Birth control dates back to the Second Millennium B.C. Egyptians used crocodile dung as vaginal spermicide. (Whether this discouraged the sperm or the sperm owner is unclear.) Greeks later used the rhythm method, magical amulets, and contraceptive potions.

Despite this context, the Bible gives no birth-control prohibition. Sex is presented as good, for pleasure not just procreation. Song of Songs, the biblical love poem, muses, "Your body is like a palm and your breasts like clusters of fruit. I will climb the palm tree and take hold of its fruit." Amen!

Prudish theologians preferred stoical philosophy to scriptural texts. The Roman Stoic Musonius Rufus taught that sex for procreation was good, but sex for pleasure was not—procreation: yes, recreation: no. (Collegiate Greek fraternities would later reverse this.) St. Jerome quoted the Stoic Seneca and altered his Bible translation to condemn contraception. St. Ambrose suggested Song of Songs be read allegorically as conversation between God and Church. (Personally, I find a spicy Bible less troubling than God talking kinky to the Church, but hey, that's just me.)

St. Augustine is the doctrine's main source. At eighteen, he got his girlfriend pregnant and joined a cult. This bizarre group considered the physical world demonic and birthing kids into it evil; members had coitus interuptus orgies, eating bread made from grain and semen.

Augustine's mom overlooked such toga yoga and avant-garde cuisine but rejected his underclass fiancé. After a ten-year relationship, he dumped her (the mistress not his mom). Regretting this decade of decadence (the sex not his callousness), he entered a socially acceptable engagement and a holy, wholly loveless marriage. The reformed party-animal reached a conclusion shared by many clergy-types: "If I can't have fun sex, no one should."

Auggy only knew two ways to do the wild thing: contraceptive tag-team lust-fest and procreative matrimonial duty. Roman society had zero population growth, so family planning never occurred to him. Converting to Catholicism, he denounced birth-control practices. Like a zealous former alcoholic, he exchanged cultic coitus interuptus for interfering with everyone else's coitus instead.

Maybe this man should not determine contraceptive usage. (Maybe he should have been encouraged to seek professional help.) Nevertheless, as the Vatican reassures the world that child-molesting priests are the exception, its birth-control policy—bringing poverty and suffering to the world's children—is still the rule.

A shoulder tap ended my visions. Palenque security politely hustled me down from the tower. I drove away as charcoal skies split open and poured. Amidst the monsoon, the outline of a boy appeared, holding his little sister with one hand and offering a pineapple for sale with the other.

I brooded to the melancholy Zen of the wipers. How long, how long, before religion 'fesses up to yet another historical "Oops"? Change comes slow, but it does come. A century ago, putting priests and pedophiles in the same title might have seemed irreverent; today, it seems closer to redundant.

Flew past a woman lighting a candle in a roadside shrine. Perhaps she was praying for her children: "Our Father, who art in heaven …" Perhaps she was praying for her priests: "Father, forgive them, for they know not what they do."

Booze, Blues & Bible-bangers

New Orleans is where the Bible belt comes unbuckled. I realize this on Bourbon Street when a black transsexual offers me his unconscious, whiskey-drenched sister for a ten-dollar blowjob or a twenty-dollar screw. Suddenly an all-white jazz band appears. Clarinets, saxophones, trumpets, trombones, banjos, and drums pummel the tragic siblings with "When the Saints Go Marching In."

Race, rye, and religion are constant themes on the Mississippi. In the American Odyssey, Huck Finn and sidekick Jim float downriver to escape racism, alcoholism, and fundamentalism. One thing is as clear as the water is muddy: they went the wrong way. Now I, Huckleberry Lyn, am heading upriver in search of some answers and the ever-elusive freedom.

Exit the French Quarter to what was once Storyville. Here jazz was born and named for the jasmine aura of the local whorehouses. I step into a bistro for red beans and rice with turnip greens. My food tastes like history—an edible incarnation of bygone days and neighborhood spirits. In nearby dirt alleys, the hungry, seven-year-old son of a prostitute once dragged around a coal cart. Jailed by age eleven for firing a pistol in New Year's Eve revelry, the boy was taken from the only family he'd ever known to reform school. Solace took the shape of a silver trumpet. Though as entitled to bitterness as anyone ever was, Louis Armstrong set out to give the world a hug instead.

Satchel-mouthed "Satchmo" single-handedly invented improvisation and swing time. His "West End

Blues" has been called the most perfect three minutes of music ever made. When his sheet music fell off during recording, he introduced America to the scat. He crooned "La Vie En Rose" with enough romantic charm to make cats kiss dogs. His canonical rendition of "What a Wonderful World" has done more to combat global misery than World Vision. Plus, forty years after redefining music, the aging master still bumped the unsoulful Beatles down the charts to make "Hello Dolly" number one in the nation.

Despite his triumphs, when Louie returned to New Orleans for Mardi gras, community and religious leaders banned his racially integrated group from performing. Heartbroken, he scrapped plans to be buried here in his hometown. Though his favorite song was "Sleepytime Down South," Armstrong chose to spend his eternal rest up North. Haunting lyrics still reflect his great soul and his suffering: "My only sin, is my skin. Why must I be so black and blue?"

Later in the day, a telecom company VP invites me to RSVP to watch a football game ASAP from their Superdome balcon de VIP. The Saints play horribly. The sinners are much more fun: our catered gluttony includes jambalaya, gumbo, etouffée, muffulettas, every local longneck beer, and every imported single-malt Scotch. Gentlemen wear khaki trousers and blue oxfords. Ladies wear huge diamonds and large breasts with the former looking genuine.

No one follows the game. Latecomers invariably ask the score only to hear awkward silence then a backslapping executive slur out, "Hell, I dunno! D'jou come ta talk er drink?" The corporation thoughtfully reduced liability by providing rooms just across a walkway at the Hyatt. When the stadium staff informs us the game has long ended, our swaggering, staggering crew stumbles to bed.

Next day, I leave Creole N'AW-lins, driving through Cajun country. Cajun is short for Acadian. Acadian is short for "a bayou-dwellin' French-Canadian with an accordion."

These folks have had it rough. Driven from France to Nova Scotia by hardship, then South to Louisiana by British, they got their fishin' nets, washin' boards, and moonshinin' stills set up just in time for Napoleon to sell their new home to the Americans for pocket change. The final insult came when McDonald's announced the new Cajun McChicken sandwich. Now, I see with my own eyes how les miserables have been driven to the point of actually enjoying country music. Somebody oughta do somethin'.

A roadside eatery boasts, "Seafood buffet: crawfish, frog legs, and alligator soup—technically inaccurate, but I guess "swamp smorgasbord" wouldn't sound tasty. I step inside for directions. Wood-carved signage reminds gentlemen to remove their hats out of respect for the ladies. However, muddy boots, greasy overalls, and tobacco-stuffed, toothpick-dangling mouths are apparently considered a tribute to the aforementioned babes.

In one corner, a massive singer fronts a rockin' zydeco band. Each time he belts the hook, "Born on a Bayou," his body squats down to spew the lyric, his face turns purple implying a hernia in progress, his superfluous flesh rolls with the downbeat, and his arm flies back to yank blue jeans up over freshly exposed ass-cleavage. Damn, he's good!

Back on the Mississippi, cypress-crowded basins give way to oak-dotted plantations. Palatial estates recall one of the world's last medieval societies. Within their walls, white knights and damsels lived by a code of honor and chivalry. Alas, this didn't extend to the surrounding fields where fellow humans died under a code of barbarism and slavery. *Gone with the Wind*? One can only hope.

Antebellum Natchez rises up ahead on the river bluff. Cock-on-the-Walk Restaurant serves me catfish, coleslaw, pickled onions, and hushpuppies, then a landmark bed & breakfast surrounds me with fine antiques and plush pillows. Slumber comes nice and easy. Rosy-fingered dawn goes unnoticed, but smoky-tentacled bacon taps me on the shoulder and pulls me down the hallway. I drive off greatly full and fully grateful.

The road forks at D'Evereaux Drive, where people were once yoked together like cattle and auctioned off. I park and stand a while. When the biblical villain Cain asserted he wasn't his brother's keeper, God responded, "Listen! Your murdered brother's blood cries out from the ground." The blood of slaves has long cried out from the dirt on which I stand. Such cries carried on Natchez blues radio WMIS directly cross-river where rockabilliest Jerry Lee Lewis was born.

While trying to become a preacher at Southwestern Bible Institute, Jerry was asked to play the song, "My God is Real" during worship. He pounded it out boogie-woogie style and was promptly expelled. They didn't want God that real. Lewis then applied his "great balls of fire" to something less original in the Deep South: tickling both "the ivories" and "the ebonies" as pianist and patron at Nellie Jackson's Natchez bawdy house, then marrying over half a dozen women, including his thirteen-year-old cousin.

Traditional religion had no place for black music. Yet there was plenty of room in the fold for the white sheep of the family, Jerry's other cousin: Jimmy Swaggart. (Before Jimmy and Jerry were scandalized by sex and rock-n-roll, federal agents arrested their fathers for distilling the local drug of choice, corn whisky.) Lewis did eventually get to preach his own prophetic message, "There's a whole lotta shakin' goin' on." As Plato wrote, "A society's foundations shake when musical style changes." Here on highway 61, where I'm cruising along toward Memphis, the world got "all shook up."

Vicksburg hits me like a brick wall. Or rather, its 17,000 Civil War graves do. This final bastion of the Confederacy, guarding the continent's main arterial waterway, held the high ground against Ulysses S. Grant's stranglehold siege to the virtual last man. Sweet magnolias scent the air as a permanent funereal bouquet.

How does one internalize such mass sacrifice on such minute terrain? I envision legions of starving, sickly adolescents laying down their lives for some personalized conception of freedom—a country free from slavery or a homeland free from federalism or just a conscience free from accusations of cowardice. They lined up to exchange flesh and blood for ideas and emotions. People long for freedom; war craves youth for its valor and naiveté. Warriors must believe they fight on moral high ground. My veteran neighbor, Jim Shaw, wears a belt buckle he took off a dead Nazi. The back is inscribed: "God is with us!"

I leave the profound silence of the battlefield for the mindless din of a riverboat casino near Greenville. Lose a couple bucks on roulette. For most locals, gambling is either a major thrill or a mortal sin. For me, it's just a tax on folks who can't do math. I'm soon back on the road.

From Vicksburg to Memphis, the Mississippi Delta was once a vast swamp of gum trees, panthers, snakes, mosquitoes, and malaria. For eons, the great muddy river gently deposited dirt on the site. Now, it is a land of rich black soil and poor black people, of fat white cotton bolls and fat white cotton bosses. The population is around 80% black. The landscape is awash in shotgun shacks without plumbing or electricity.

Ironically, a century ago, as diminishing crops were being carefully weighed and sold, a priceless musical harvest sprung up unnoticed, then scattered its seeds to the wind and the Windy City. Chester Arthur Burnett's story is somewhat typical of the region's legendary bluesmen.

Chester, aka Howlin' Wolf, was born in 1910 on the Illinois Central train line near the Mississippi/Alabama border. His eighteen-year-old, Black, sharecropper dad married his fifteen-year-old, Choctaw, pregnant mom unceremoniously.

During his toddler years, his father moved away, his native grandfather nicknamed him "Wolf" for his mischievousness, and his mother threw him out to fend for himself. He found shelter with his brutal, violent uncle—a church deacon. His new guardian leather-whipped him into working cotton from sunup to bedtime while providing him with bread, milk, and eventually a pair of shoes.

Chester whistled or sang while plowing. During breaks, he beat on a bucket or made a one-string diddley-bow out of board and bailing wire. After saving for and donning his first pair of trousers, he was knocked into mud and slop by the family's prize hog. He beat the pig to death, then ran for the train, just ahead of uncle's whip—barefoot, raggedy, thirteen, and Delta-bound.

On the Young & Morrow Plantation, he slaved behind a team of flea-bitten, farting mules. The blues, a series of twelve-bar phrases based on three chords, an A-A-B rhyme pattern, and simple, passionate truth, came as naturally as sweating. The music was a road out of hell. It provided escape during work, relaxation after work, and with mastery a way to quit work.

Chester played Delta juke joints with mentor Charlie Patton and pal Robert Johnson. These hangouts were dangerous outfits where bluesmen brought in the women, women brought in the men, and men, drinking whisky from bottles or tin cups while packing guns or knives, gambled with deadly intensity.

Under the scorching sun, Chester grew into a six foot, five inch tall, almost three hundred hulking pound adult with huge head, hands, and feet. His skin was smooth and dark. His blue-gray eyes, growly voice, and paranoid/sexually predatory nature truly seemed wolfish.

Onstage, Chester beat his guitar like a drum and rode it like a pony. He bent strings with his fingers or made them sob with a slide. He played one harmonica with his mouth and another simultaneously with his nose. He padded around like a caged animal or crawled across the floor. He licked his lips, humped the air, stared balefully, mumbled to himself, and always carried a pistol.

In Clarksdale, I visit the Delta Blues Museum to research more on Howlin' Wolf. At Boss Hawg's Barbeque, I perform last rites on swine that stains my clothes like Chester's nemesis. (Of all the things that damage the heart, I regret pulled pork and torrid love the least.) I reach Beale Street and Sun Studios in Memphis with mind and body still digesting.

In the 1950s, Chester Burnett played on Beale Street while a teenage Elvis Presley hung in the shadows. The Wolf also preceded the King into Sun Studios, recording his masterpieces, "Moanin' at Midnight" and "Smokestack Lightnin'." On the latter, hypnotic rhythm gradually picks up steam like a locomotive. Full-moon falsetto-howls punctuate work-song field-holler vocals. Dark, cryptic lyrics convey a Gothic spirituality and summon up ghost trains from his disturbed nightmarish childhood near the tracks. All throughout, Wolf's primal soul wails for his mother like a lupine cub lost in the wilderness.

This theme of "a woman done him wrong" permeates Chester's musicology. In real life, his mother refused to speak to him. Neither his serial adulteries nor her child abandonment troubled her much, but his playing the devil's music (blues) in places serving demonic drink (alcohol) was inexcusable. She insisted that she was Jesus' child but that he had sold his soul.

Near the end of his life, he tracked her down in Clarksdale and hugged her, slipping a five-hundred-dollar bill into her pocket. She found it, spat on it, stomped on it, and yelled, "I don't want your dirty money!" He cried all the way to Memphis.

In his tormented classic, "Goin' Down Slow," Chester begs for pardon: "Please, write my mama. Tell her the shape I'm in. Tell her to pray for me: forgive me for my sin." Wolf always remained skeptical of organized religion; he figured if his mom and uncle were on that side, he belonged on the other. Yet he knelt by his bed in prayer every night. British bandleader Chris Barber hosted blues and gospel musicians for decades and recalled, "The only one who ever said grace before meals was Wolf, the only one!"

When his kidneys failed, he phoned mom from his Chicago deathbed. She refused to take the call.

Religion's designation of blues and later rock 'n' roll as "devil music" was a thin disguise for its real crime of being "nigger music." (WC Handy, first great composer of the blues, was a pious bible-believer who wrote uplifting songs.) The contagious groove and earthy lyrics were commonly attributed to the "primitiveness" of the black race. However, primitive nature was not the muse, primitive treatment was. Reduce people to survival level and they confront life's elemental themes and rawest emotions. In parlor talk, "Necessity is the mother of invention." In the Delta, it's just a mean motherfucker.

Chester once told an interviewer, "The people that come up the hard way—that come up sufferin'—they can play that music. You think the blues is gone down for the count? Blues is gonna be played in people's homes. Even to this day, I wouldn't be allowed in their houses—but my music is gonna be." Today, statues of him span the length of the Mississippi and his image dons a US postage stamp. Now everyone plays music from the Delta, but not just anyone can put the Delta into the music.

I sit in the lavishly elegant lobby of the Memphis Peabody Hotel. Mallards splash softly in the marble fountain. Lovebirds playfully tinkle at the grand piano. My request for whisky without a glass is refused, until I explain my desire to toast Howlin' Wolf. As if by hoodoo, a bottle, a gathering, and even a harmonica materialize. An intimate fellowship descends upon the room and prevails unto the wee hours.

In the morning, I do Graceland—the Taj Mahal of tacky—architectural proof that the unexamined life can be worth living, if you've got the cash. Elvis was as unrefined as he was charismatic. Like the Great Gatsby, he remade himself into a squire but really only convinced his "po' white trash" brethren. He found rising from dirt-poor son of a bootlegger to filthy-rich king of rock 'n' roll much easier than rising above class snobbery.

When bought by Presley in 1957, Graceland stood on Bellevue Boulevard a couple miles north of the Mississippi line, at the border between the impoverished rural South of his upbringing and the bustling redneck metropolis of Memphis, where the first drive-in movie, motel chain, and supermarket were born. The roadway was renamed Elvis Presley Boulevard over the loud protests of the non-rockin' Bellevue Baptist Church, whose thousands of mostly-white members have since fled to suburbia, leaving Graceland an outpost in drugland.

The location as a hilltop showcase on a busy thoroughfare was intentional. Elvis wanted adoration but not invasion. His see-over stone wall and see-through wrought-iron, music-note gates were designed to remind the simplest fan, "Me: Elvis, you: tourist, look but don't enter." The King's relatives formed a homey but firm security force. The physical site and retention of the old "Graceland" name reflected the heavenward hymn, "I've got a mansion, just over the hilltop," which Elvis tearily quavered out on his 1961 gospel album.

The overdone white columns, pediment, and façade echo the then current fetish for the umpteenth re-release of "Gone With the Wind." The film saga became a national epic, transforming the American Dream from "a chicken in every pot" to "a column on every portico." Depression era need was replaced by modern consumer greed. The manse itself was constructed of stone from Elvis' birthplace Tupelo, bricks from Mississippi mud, and timber from Delta swamps. Home is where the heart is and when Elvis' heart wasn't in some Vegas showgirl's pants, it was here.

The mega-columns may also have offered a retort to Northeastern elitists who ridiculed him as a country bumpkin. A year before the property purchase, NBC's Steve Allen Show made Elvis sing Big Mama Thornton's classic, "Hound Dog," to a slouching basset hound in front of classical columns. The intent was to reveal his "uncultured" Negro music for what it was. In contrast, "classy" non-hillbilly guest Milton Berle joked about being Presley's long-lost twin (who was tragically stillborn) and performed his lame transvestite shtick to "enlightened" approval. Elvis was humiliated. The next morning, after a gander at the ratings, former critic Ed Sullivan offered him the highest fee ever paid for a TV gig. The language of black music was foreign to the establishment, but money was their mother tongue.

I step into the foyer. Inside, Graceland is like a Hollywood set with disposable (albeit expensive) rotating furnishings and theme rooms. The front half of the house presents ceremonial, image-projecting space; the back half features functional, chaotic sprawl.

On my left is the dining area. White carpet surrounds a glass table and black upholstered chairs resting on marble floor. To my right is the living room. Plump damask chairs and a fifteen-foot white couch face a stone fireplace to rival *Citizen Kane*. The music room extension displays a genuine gold piano. Above me, a chandelier illuminates a gilded staircase with golden balusters. The top landing leads into the royal playboy pad, then the infamous throne room/death potty.

I descend to the basement. A pool table fills a chamber where walls and ceiling are made from mass quantities of pleated Indian-paisley fabric forming a tent. The mood is warm, organic and hippy. Adjacent is a blue and yellow cubical with mirrored ceiling, lightening-bolt wall-mural, and NASA-mission-control bank of TVs for simultaneous viewing. The ambience is cool, angular and art deco.

An oh-so-private deluxe home bar equipped for serious drinking contrasts starkly with the oh-so-religious younger Elvis who wouldn't be seen in a Nashville pub to check out a band with his agent. Of course this wasn't the only time that fundamentalist rules produced more hypocrisy than moderation. However, it may have been the first case to go out in a milkshaked, cheeseburgered, prescription-drugged, liquored-up blaze of glory.

I proceed to the den—a legendary eyesore. After Presley's death, the monstrosity was nicknamed "the jungle room" for tours, to make the décor seem meaningful rather than embarrassing, a little gag not a big gaffe, like a brief rainforest intermission from Priscilla's palatable palace. Yet, no bullshit can explain this dogshit! Here Elvis repeatedly shot out the TV set when Robert Goulet or Mel Tormé came on. Here also a friend installed the waterfall (with plastic hoses still visible) that shorted out and flamed up during a 1971 Christmas party, until the family sledgehammered the wall wiring.

During Elvis' funeral, Carolyn Kennedy (another booze smuggler's progeny) visited Graceland for a "condolence call." The family thought it was a sort of state visit and ushered her into this room, where they were grieving privately and inconsolably. Ms. Kennedy noted the decorating instead.

She rushed Rolling Stone a stunned story about the tasteless Polynesian Primitive décor, which included mahogany paneling, floor and ceiling green shag carpet, Wookie-fur lampshades, plastic hanging vines, and chain-saw-sculpted pine thrones. In short, Elvis' lack of sophistication had once again been pointed out by a Yankee elitist as lacking in scruples as he was in class. Jungle motif meets savage tactics.

Perhaps the raunchy room was a defiant joke on the world, a man's primal rebel yell against fashion magazine interviews, Priscilla's syrupy domestications, and clergymen who dubbed rock 'n' roll as faddish jungle music. The 1970s Vegas show included the lyric, "I'm the king of the jungle." While Elvis' pelvis no longer shocks the world's sensibilities, his polyurethane-coated myrtle wood coffee table still does. Rock on Elvis!

Today, when most Presley recordings sound like the Fonz singing with a barbershop quartet, it's hard to grasp how they were once the vinyl incarnation of multi-ethnic hipness and teenage rebellion. Yet it's so. Defying religiously buttressed prejudice, he united black and white teens into a single musical tradition—a pretty spiritual accomplishment for a not-so-spiritual guy.

I pass through the trophy hall, full of gold records and jeweled jumpsuits, to the meditation garden. The spot harbors a mishmash of angels, goddesses, and faux-classical columns with some upside down. Elvis constructed the shrine during a brief period of spiritual searching. His friends laughed. Religiousness is expected in the Bible belt; spirituality is not. The King's grave is also here. He lies between a Jesus statue and a flickering flame, betwixt heaven and hell, just as he lived in turmoil between religion and hedonism. I pause, reflecting on my own thirst for something that transcends both.

Departing Memphis, I stop at Mud Island to pull off my shoes and wade down the mile-long, several-inch-deep cement-and-water topographical model of the Mississippi. Sounds silly, but it's a fast and fun geography course not to be missed. The only question the museum doesn't answer is whether the crowd lying around drunk at the New Orleans end are tourists or part of the replica.

Driving over the real Mississippi, I glance back at the glistening Memphis Pyramid. The monument offers a proud comparison to the city's namesake on the Nile. It entreats the beholder to only partly remember two great civilizations, both built alongside rivers and on the backs of forced laborers. I discard all serious thought at a mid-bridge sign reading, "Welcome to Arkansas: home of Bill Clinton."

Speed past West Memphis: dirt, dust, truck stops, moon pies, and RC Colas. Take US 55 North traversing hazy rice fields and catfish farms. Twist the radio: Jesus, Shania, quilting, fertilizer, blessed silence.

Nearing Sikeston, Missouri, miles and miles of billboards foretell the "Home of Throwed Rolls." The promised miracle turns out to be a diner where if you hold up your finger a distant waiter tosses you a bun, where anything that can be fried has been, and where macaroni and cheese count as one side-vegetable. Actually, like the previously glorified barbeque, if you're gonna die from somethin', this is a fine way to go.

The highway, to which I return in a gaseous, bloated stupor, could be called the "Home of Throwed Souls." An exodus of Southern blacks to Chicago along this stretch in the 1940s and 50s was one of the largest peacetime migrations in history, often compared with the flight of Jews from Egyptian bondage to the Promised Land. Perhaps the preservation of blues is a holy rite akin to the celebration of Passover.

The threadbare road joins parallel black threads, until finally merging with a big, tangled knitting-ball of freeways. Saint Louis is gateway to the North, where the Blues is a hockey team, not a way of life. In this freer metropolis, over a century ago, black composer Scott Joplin could emerge as the American Chopin and even produce operas. His ragtime classics such as "The Entertainer," "Easy Winners," and "Maple Leaf Rag," blend raucous frolics with deep sentimental longings, symphonic elegance with chromatic hints of down-and-dirty blues.

Joplin took black syncopations into the cultured salons of the world, demolishing the long-held truism that music was a hierarchy of virtue descending from the European to the darker races. Even so, the Sedalia Maple Leaf Club—a respectable black-owned fraternal organization for which Scott named his masterwork—was perpetually harassed by local churches for allowing liquor, playing cards, and (worst of all) interracial dating. The biblical witness that Jesus distributed wine, Moses married an African, and Apostle Peter used games of chance didn't slow their zeal to shut down this musical heritage site. Apparently, waltzes can be "devil music," too.

I take the Anheuser-Busch tour of the planet's biggest brewery, then visit a church housing the world's largest Byzantine mosaic collection. One pope called it "the greatest cathedral of the Americas"—the church, not the brewery. Being a renaissance man, I test the acoustic reaction of the colossal space to whistling the Budweiser jingle. (Yep, I'm goin' straight to hell.) In the shadowy, stained-glass stillness, I once again ponder the alternative to stuffy religion or empty hedonism. There must be a better way. Perhaps I can gain a higher perspective from a loftier vantage point.

Long before the banks of the new world Nile thrust up a triangular pharaoh-phallus at Memphis, they hoisted a kinder, gentler geometric. The Saint Louis Arch is a graceful, unimposing curve of shimmering steel—unless you ascend over 600 feet inside the creaking, swaying, sculpture/carnival-ride. From the apex, my eyes can see much more than my stomach would prefer.

Across the river is East St. Louis. In this violent slum, Howlin' Wolf and Albert King had a knock-down drag-out brawl as band members, who kept their guns so close that one blew off a testicle while drumming, got sent to the hospital trying to break it up. In this same ghetto, Scott Joplin had to debut his first opera under deplorable conditions. Turns out the white folks only wanted to hear his "satanic stuff" after all. (Lucky break for the soon-to-be-spawned, classically untrained luciferites: John, Paul, George, and Ringo.)

Off to the North is Hannibal, birthplace of Mark Twain. According to Hemingway, all of American literature descends from Twain. Most of Twain descends from this river. Across the panorama before me, Huck and Jim and every reader's inner child make their great escape from the shackles of this world. On one of these marshy islands, Jim, the runaway-slave-within-us-all, comments, "I's rich now, come to look at it. I owns mysef, en I's wuth eight hund'd dollars." How many of us truly own ourselves or even grasp the value of such ownership?

Above all, the arch now making me queasy celebrates St. Louis as gateway to the West. The Mississippi—badly pronounced Chippewa for "Great River"—once marked the line between civilized East and wild frontier. St. Louis boasted the first railway bridge to span the mighty flow. The city also stands at the confluence of the Missouri. Had this westward fork been called the Mississippi, the whole would constitute the world's longest river. Instead, Jack Kerouac called her a muddy poem flowing through the heart of a vast country where a tree falling in Montana can drift to the sea. (Warning: this description is nearly worthless and sounds goofy when used to ask directions.)

In 1804, Meriwether Lewis and William Clark set out from here to investigate the Missouri in all its glory. I freely admit that following their route on four wheels and asphalt is grossly anticlimactic. However, after too many years of too many beers, Chicago nightlife appeals little more than Southern religion. So, I defrost a poem flowing from the heart of my muddled schooldays and take the river less traveled by hoping that will make all the difference.

Crossing the Great Plains, one can feel small and windblown. I spot coyote, antelope, jackrabbits, prairie dogs, and even a distant tornado. As daylight wanes, rolling hills and boundless horizon give way to a dazzlingly clear and starry sky. Past Sioux City, Iowa, I toss my sleeping bag onto the land of the Lakota and drift away, counting phantom buffalo and ghostly hunters.

Up and gone with a fireball sunrise, I pull over near Bismarck, North Dakota to pee in complete isolation where Mandan farming villages were once more populous than St. Louis. Drive and drive and drive to a funny-smell-motel-from-hell. Drive some more. Just short of deciding to give up the plains crossing and homestead for the winter, I reach Great Falls, Montana. The thundering cascade is 300 yards wide and 80 feet high and conceals more falls behind and more behind those. Here, Lewis and Clark's expedition had to abandon river and portage overland. So would I. Here also, their whisky supply ran out. Alas, my cache of wry tales of rye would soon be restocked.

Bearing Northwest, I sojourn in a small valley where the Shoshone once hid from the well-horsed and heavily armed Blackfoot. A current resident named Eldon still lives in fear, but it's hellhounds not warriors on his trail. When Lewis-and-Clark-companion John Colter ran naked for many miles ahead of pursuing Blackfoot, he stumbled into a "hell of steam and boiling mud": Yellowstone. Eldon has been fleeing the dogs for years, stumbling into his own personal hell. His wife serves me Huckleberry muffins.

"What do you do, Eldon?"

"I'm second shift foreman at the mill."

"How 'bout you, Bev?"

"I stay busy with my church." She lays her head on his shoulder. "I wish he'd go with me, but he prefers not to."

"How come?"

He pauses long, running a trembling hand through sparse white hair. "I guess I'm just destined for hell." His soft matter-of-fact voice contradicts his terrified look.

"Why do you say that?"

He sighs. "Way back in the war, we captured some Japanese prisoners." His voice quivers. "Sarge showed us how to get 'em to talk." His eyes tear up. "I didn't want to do it, but I was afraid." He sobs. "So, I joined in. I guess unless I get saved, I'm toast."

"What holds you back?"

"When I married Bev, we agreed I wouldn't drink but that every year on our anniversary we'd sit outside to watch the sunset and share a bottle of wine."

"And … ?"

"I've kept both commitments, always will, but most folks at that church drive over to Idaho to buy their liquor where no one knows. I know 'cuz I see 'em. You can't be a hypocrite if you wanna follow God. Honesty is all I got left to give. So, I guess I'm finished …" Coughing and crying, he stumbles off to be alone.

Bev offers me another muffin.

Approaching the Canadian border, I skid over an icy fogbound pass into the remote Yaak Valley. A steamy river-marsh winds through wilderness past the rusted-out metal of the Dirty Shame Saloon. The pub's name comes from a favorite tune of Son House, who vacillated between bluesman and preacher. Seems the long arm of religion even reaches here. I stop for a brew.

The leathery face of a much-tattooed barmaid is crisscrossed with dark crevices mirroring the deep cleavage that plunges into her unbuttoned denim shirt. The jukebox is playing ZZ Top blues …

"Jesus just left Chicago and he's bound for New Orleans."

Mark Twain once quipped, "If Christ were here now, there's one thing he would not be: a Christian."

"Took a jump through Mississippi, muddy water turned to wine."

Whether Jesus will return to perform this miracle, I don't know. If he does, one thing is certain: the fundamentalists will crucify him again.

Of Elephants & Men

India seems great until the eunuch curses my genitals. As I board a rickshaw in the village of Mahabalipuram, a hermaphrodite approaches and begins touching me all over with one hand while rubbing my scalp with the other. Such people are considered good luck here. Their touch constitutes a blessing when responded to with a donation. Still, this fortunate and auspicious moment exceeds my comfort zone.

Though I ramp up the firmness of my "Thanks but no thanks," he/she increases the frenzy of his/her anatomical tour. Like a cheerleader on prom night, I sweetly but doggedly stick to my "No means no." Finally, the eunuch grunts in disgust, taps my crotch with a shamanistic gesture, and stomps away. Thus commences my long-envisioned spiritual pilgrimage on the subcontinent. So far, nothing has shriveled up or fallen off. I'll keep you posted on that.

Checking into the Sterling Beach Resort, I slouch over to their Pongamiya Restaurant for breakfast. Idlys are the local delicacy. These fermented rice cakes are served with a coconut, green chili, and mustard seed chutney, as well as a lentil, red chili, and vegetable stew called Sambar. Heavenly flavor and hellacious heat. Sipping the combination of black tea, milk, sugar, and spices known as Chai Masala, I listen to the crashing surf for a long time. Getting started is the hardest part of these pilgrimage things.

Eventually, I head out across the burning sands of town. Mahabalipuram was the ancient seaport of the Pallava Kings between the 3rd and 8th centuries AD. They left behind a breathtaking cluster of monolithic shrines, structural stone temples, and cut caves with granite bas reliefs. These sacred sites are devoted to the Hindu Trinity of Creator Brahma, Sustainer Vishnu, and Destroyer Shiva. Fabulous rock sculptures of jolly reclining Ganesh and buxom sensual Laksmi are for sale everywhere.

The current population—or midday's children, in Salman Rushdie speak—are mostly black-skinned, Tamil-speaking people. The women wear elegant silk saris and often keep a conservative distance from interaction with men. There is a shocking prevalence of filthy, maimed or deformed youngsters, who cling onto me for blocks, until and after I give them food. They are snarky and confrontational, because they live in a desperate game where the easily-dissuaded beggar goes hungry. I hustle through these precious but ill-valued gems of the present to see the highly acclaimed stones of the past. No doubt future generations will dodge their dirty starving kids to see our dusty crumbling bricks with only a similar melancholy reflection as the wheel of suffering or samsara turns.

Just as my sweat drainage overflows my boots, I reach a group of pagoda-shaped shrines chiseled out of huge boulders. They are referred to as the Five Rathas. These monoliths are carved up into pavilions with columns and niches for divine statues. The lofty tops take the form of pyramids, pull carts, and thatched huts. Stone lions and elephants stand guard. My gawking at the wonder of this intricate holy art lasts as long as my impending sunstroke will allow. I regretfully retreat north about 200 meters to the shade of the park-like central hillside.

For the next few hours, I trek around the swaying trees and chattering monkeys of the hillock from cave to cave. Each alcove holds a rock mural worthy of the Louvre. The mythology splayed before my wide eyes includes goddess Durga battling the buffalo-headed demon, Vishnu's boar avatar rescuing mother earth from the sea, and Lord Krishna lifting a mountain to protect a pastoral community from

Varuna the rain. These panoramas tucked into the darkened recesses are like stone cinema. The mere sight of Lakshmi sitting on a lotus and bathed by two elephants has me seriously contemplating the feasibility of having relations with a wall.

Speaking of great walls, I now stand before India's answer to China's. It's 43 feet high and 96 feet long. It has an off-colored cleft from top to bottom, which functions compositionally as the Ganga descending from heaven. (Calm down Bob Marley fans; that's a river.) It has gods, demi-gods, nagas, nymphs, sages, warriors, and all God's creatures rushing to see and drink from the font of life. It is cool and beautiful and the apex of Dravidian art. You stand and you stare and your mouth hangs open and you try to burn it on the back of your mind for recall the rest of your life—and then I go back to the hotel cause I'm hungry.

Lounging poolside and wearing the minimum allowed by law, I indulge in the potato-spinach-peanut-and-spice-filled pastries called samosas. The saltiness demands an ice-cold Kingfisher beer. Along comes Tandoori Chicken marinated in yogurt and spices then skewered and cooked in a clay oven. The saltiness demands another ice-cold Kingfisher beer. Arguably India's best brew, what it lacks in flavor it makes up for in refreshment. By the time the bill arrives, I gaze skeptically at the high bottle count but in no condition to challenge a waiter who doubtless has a PhD in mathematics and a moral revulsion to strong drink.

Strolling up the coast instead, I come to the majestic Shore Temple. This massive two-spired structure has paved forecourts lined with Brahma bulls and a look of perfect aesthetic harmony. I sit down on the beach near the monument to watch the sun set and commune with the infinite.

The next morning, I take the 50 kilometer bus ride north to Chennai. At City Center, I shop in Landmark Bookstore to buy some classic Indian movies—Lagaan and Ghajini starring Aamir Khan plus the Fire, Earth, and Water Trilogy directed by Deepa Mehta. The mall also has a renowned vegetarian restaurant: Sangeetha's. I have mixed raitha (yogurt, tomatoes, cucumbers, carrots, and onions) and palak paneer (spinach with cheese cubes) over basmati rice. The meal ends with a betel leaf filled with dried cherries and cumin for a digestive aid with a mild narcotic effect.

Spend my afternoon at Kapaleeswarar Temple. You enter this ancient Hindu house of worship by removing your shoes then walking under a towering sloped roof carved with thousands of brightly-colored and multi-tiered mythological figures. The astonishing miniature horde tells the spiritual tales of several millennia. Inside, you line up to pray before the welcoming elephant Ganesh, after which a priest marks your forehead with ashes from a sacred fire. The crowd is packed. People slowly migrate around the courtyard circle, performing various ritual devotions at the many shrines.

Three times, I try to meld with the throng pressing into the Hindus-only inner sanctum. Three times, some self-appointed temple bouncers boot my butt out. While a very-Catholic Latino girl nearby has no trouble entering or staying, whiteness and tallness defeat all my attempts to quietly and reverently go with the flow. My honest-but-hedgy explanations that I am "more or less a devotee" or "a student of all spirituality" get me nowhere. The young male zealots who evict me clearly didn't learn their Hinduism from California hippies. Nevertheless, the last time they catch me, I am already in the Holy of Holies, so I consider my browns-only party crashing a sort of quest fulfilled. Think of me what you will, I got to be in the dark-smoky-moldy-holy place for two seconds and you didn't.

My rejection by Hindus gives me a taste for Islam. I have dinner at Daawat Kebab Shop in Adyar. The plump Muslim owner greets me with a warm smile between his chocolate bald head and cottony white beard. He brings baskets of warm chewy Naan bread. His black lentil Dhal

Makhani bubbles with ghee and spices. Yet nothing compares to the Kalmi Kebab chicken marinated in mint sauce. I gorge myself with unrestrained orgasmic groans. I suppress an urge to shout, "There is no God but Allah!" I leave in a glowing gaseous stupor.

Across the hall is the café Cup 'n' Saucer. Plop down on their sofa, surrounded by lime green walls and brown leather bean bags, to drink some of the world's finest black tea from Darjeeling while watching the cricket match on TV. As night falls, I head for what is probably Chennai's most revered sacred site.

The Basilica of Saint Thomas has a historical claim to have been the burial place of one of Jesus' twelve apostles. The evidence for this is vastly greater than that for the Vatican claim of the Apostle Peter being buried in Rome or the Dan Brown claim of Jesus' descendants being alive in France. Apparently due to the missionary efforts of Thomas, there were thousands of disciples in India before there were any in most of Europe. Just as the Jewishness of Jesus was long deemphasized by many Europeans, so were his multitudes of "dark children" often left off the Eurocentric maps of Christendom.

I feel a tingle as I mount the church steps. A wave of wooziness passes when I stare up the lofty spires stabbing the sky. Down the ramp into the subterranean crypt, I pad in silent expectation then take a seat in the chapel located on the spot of the ancient tomb. I pray and hope to feel more of what I think I should feel. Sometimes an old heart can seem like a dead battery that wants to fire up but just doesn't have enough juice. Perhaps, like Graham Greene, I haven't seen the power and the glory because I'm looking in the wrong sanctuary. I resolve to journey on northward to the home of a renowned animal preserve. Maybe Mother Nature will provide the recharge I seek.

Book a seat the next morning on the Coromandel Express to Visakhapatnam or Vizag for short. Riding a train across India is supposed to be one of those life-affirming experiences, right? At a minimum, it affirms that those of us who have enough food to eat and water to shower with should be more content with life than we generally are or even know how to be.

Outside the window pass thatched-roof slums, hand-painted buses, and motorcycles carrying families of four with mother sitting sideways. Meandering river washes are dotted with loinclothed bathers and flanked by laundry festooned sandbars. Water buffalo live up to their name, buried in lakes to their necks with monsoons drenching heads and horns. Remembering that today is Gandhi's birthday, I pull out his favorite text, *The Bhagavad-Gita*, for some reflective time.

Across from me sits Harshita, draped in cream colored silks, gold earrings and pearly smile flashing on black skin, her elegant form assuming a natural yoga posture as unsandaled feet sway carelessly against my leg. To my right hunches a bald man with bulging eyes, emitting a ceaseless talkstream of unsolicited geographical trivia, astrological interpretation, and medicinal superstition, which increases in intensity with each 5 rupee chai he downs.

Over the next ten hours, we cross red porous rock country with deep-green lotus-choked channels. Then come tan-stubbled basmati rice fields framed by fire-blackened palms. I believe Harshita and I communicate more with our hundred or so cautious words than is achieved by all the verbal tsunami we tune out.

The next morning serves up an elegant breakfast in the nautical-themed sitting room of the oceanside Park Hotel. The previous night's dark journey and my lovely dark Telugu companion seem like something I dreamed up. I hope not. Here, as in many places, lighter skin is associated with status and beauty. Since the supreme artist chose to paint with a diverse palette, I marvel at the audacity of the Creator's self-appointed critics. After the meal, an upper-caste woman enlightens me on local culture by stating matter-of-factly: "The Tamil and Telugu people are highly religious, because as you can see, they are black and ugly and so have little to hope for in this world." The scariest part is that her tone exudes not hate but compassion.

Stroll along the steel blue ocean and violent white surf to a sprawling park. Happy-looking families cover every blade of grass and most of the dirt patches. Masses of smiling children remind me how much fun kids used to have, before civil litigation deprived so many parks of things like sharp rusty metal and open sewage flow. I almost become nostalgic for the libertarian childhood I never had. Almost.

Vizag's waterfront also offers a submarine tour. This imposing black hulk was provided by the Soviet Union for the Indian Navy, during the years when the United States was allied with Pakistan. (Is it just me or does it seem like America picked the wrong dog in that fight?) Now, I'll admit touring the sub doesn't rival the grandeur of the Taj Mahal, but any guy who can look at a U-boat and not wanna go inside is gonna have to drop his pants to convince me he ever was a boy. I was, so I pay the 25 rupees with uninhibited glee.

The sub is as cool as it is predictable—millions of dials and switches to wonder about, hundreds of overheads to bang your skull on, and the ghosts of a few sailors, who lived a cramped, stinky, sometimes-oxygenless existence, so that those above they cared about might breathe as freely and long as possible.

The following day, I rent a car and drive the deliriously-winding cliffside route to the remote Aruku Valley. Stop first at the Tribal Museum. Cultural artifacts from the area's indigenous people include textiles, tools, masks, and weapons, giving a reminder how hard most people traditionally work to produce food, clothes, and necessities from scratch. How quickly we forget that those preparing food or raising children are not doing menial labor but the only stuff truly essential to the species.

Looping around the foggy fertile valley, I park at a thundering river cascade. Crowds of smiling natives stand in the shallow rushing water, making flower offerings and taking ritual baths. Apparently paradise is not lost, it's just located farther from shopping malls than many would prefer.

Before leaving Aruku, I visit Borra Caves. Deep within this netherworld of rocks and shadows, I find a spindly metal staircase ascending to the lofty ill-defined heights. Piles of sandals lie at the base as hundreds of people congest the vertical climb. Removing my footwear, I join the long line of compressed bodies, upon whom a slimy, smelly mist falls continuously. Slippery step by step, I progress imperceptibly toward the ambiguous holiness above.

Eventually I reach the cavern ceiling, where a jagged crevice entry leads to a hidden nook. The crouching resident priest dots my forehead, baptizes me with incense, and points the way for me to descend as I came, swimming against the human current I barely navigated going up. After spending half a day pressed against humanity in the dark, I decide to spend the next with animals in the sun.

Just North of Vizag, the Indira Gandhi Zoological Park blends almost seamlessly into the surrounding hills and forest. Granted: zoos are animal prisons. Still, a long hard look into crocodilian eyes reminds me that not all the incarcerated are as sweet and innocent as their advocates suggest. Some are cold-blooded killers. Plus, when given the heart-stopping treat of seeing and hearing eight huge tigers feeding around all sides of me, I conclude I will support their release only if they are not paroled into my neighborhood.

Nevertheless, when an inmate with a cruel chain on his leg puts his trunk on my shoulder, I promise I will bring his case to the attention of my readers. If anyone out there has a good plan for springing an elephant, I assure you he's all ears. I also believe he will readjust to normal civilized society, if he can just get out of the world of humans.

Mighty Ganesh is often portrayed with both an elephant and a mouse. This represents the duality of strength and humility in divine nature. Yet most human souls only seek help from above when they find themselves in vulnerable avatars like age, poverty, or sickness. The pacadermic handcuff recalled Shakespeare and Steinbeck's observation that the best-laid plans of great and small oft go astray. Why should it take a glaring clusterfuck like India to propel men toward spirituality? Why do superbowl winners say "I'm going to Disneyland," while church is a standard destination for the down and out?

Continuing north, I wind past lovely Rushikonda Beach with its symmetric waves from the Bay of Bengal. Motoring up a steep hill, I come to the sacred Buddhist site of Thotla Konda. At one time, this place held revered fragments of Siddhartha's physical body. Today, it offers a stroll around stupas, purification tanks, and brick ruins from 2,000-year-old monastic communities. Predictably for my mindset, the vast panorama of the ocean itself steals the show from the crumbling relics of religion, however holy.

Following my instinctive awe, I wander down to the water's edge. What makes this seashore feel unique? The wild random scattering of damp cubical rocks, criss-crossed with crevices like an old swami's face? The twisting miniature rivers emerging from the sand and eroding their way back down to the oneness from which they were briefly torn? The remarkably close and thunderous God-clap of the surf? Perhaps these components come together uniquely here. Yet, one thing is clearly and totally unique: who I am and where I'm at on the occasion of this ocean encounter. The vastness of the sea changes far less than we do between such meetings with the transcendent.

An inward glance reveals that I am neither depressed nor inspired but possessed of a dull contentment. The grandeur of the deep always moves me, but maybe less with each passing year. India is a favorite destination for those seeking spiritual renewal, but learning to sip chai while nearby children forage through garbage must surely produce irreversible heart damage. I begin to doubt whether all the sandalwood incense and jasmine flowers in India´s myriad temples can cover the stench of this world's evil floating up to heaven. My aging heart apparently needs two things Jesus gave Thomas: faith and wine. Continuing my seaward stare from a nearby café table, I also gaze deep into a bottle of local vintage called simply Madera. Is it good? God is good. The wine is … good enough.

Sacred Ground & Holy Water

The next time you eat salmon, you may see an apparition: a barefoot warrior with conical spruce hat, grizzly-bear-tattooed chest, and mother-of-pearl-studded cape. He's no hallucination; he's a Haida watchman, standing guard over your dinner and, perhaps, our planet. How well I remember my encounter with this guardian spirit.

We were sailing through dense fog on a drizzly night—farther north than I'd ever been before. Cloud ceiling hung low enough to make you hunch. Cloud walls, held at bay by surging and dimming deck lamps, enclosed an eerie space.

A remote coastline of moss-choked forests and deep fjords loomed without warning, then vanished without explanation. As I gripped the rail in nervous silence, my animalistic senses heightened to pick apart the sounds—ship noises, sea noises, other noises. How many creaky boats had hugged this ragged shoreline? How many timid souls had braved this fogbound strait?

First came the Haida. From ancient times, these philosophical craftsmen carved up their world into spiritual realms of earth, sea, and sky. With lofty vision, they divided themselves into raven and eagle clans. Then, lowering their gaze, they set about the tasks of life on earth, albeit the sacred earth of the islands called Haida Gwaii.

Having duly noted that nature provided four seasons and two sexes, the Haida went with the flow, both tidal and menstrual. In autumn, the women gathered kelp, roe, roots, berries, mushrooms, shellfish, cloverleaves, and crabapples.

The men, with bigger muscles and shorter attention spans, chased deer sauntering down to drink and caught salmon swimming up to spawn.

In winter, the community hibernated in post-and-beam, cedar-plank longhouses. Outside, dramatic red and black murals covered the façades. Also, front-and-center totem poles sported fierce family crests, with the bottom creature's gaping mouth forming an oval door to the smoky, fire-lit interior.

Inside, the ambience included aromatherapy (drying salmon hung from rafters) and soft rock music (sounds of malleable, black argillite being sculpted, along with interludes of grandma and grandpa getting busy under a blanket).

One can hardly overestimate the glee when spring arrived. Fertile women pierced babies' ears, tattooed children's bodies, and bathed in rushing streams, ice-cold water pouring through long, dark hair, cascading over engorged voluptuousness and funneling down into … well, you can take it from there. Meanwhile, testosterone-laden men felled towering cedars, hollowed-out canoes, and prepared to expand dominion over the third realm of sea.

Throughout summer, these ambitious mariners crisscrossed Hecate Strait, trading for eulachon oil to enrich their diet and raiding for captive slaves to enrich their economy. As I peered over the railing, straining to glimpse nearby land through thick mist and mammoth waves, the enormity of their nautical cojones shamed me.

Next came the white boys. I say "boys" because these fur-trading expeditions generally left the women at home. So, by the time they reached Haida Gwaii, the sailors hadn't erected their totem poles at the oval entrances to their favorite longhouses in quite some time. Perhaps the rise of hostilities with the Haida is less surprising than the lack of mutiny on the ships.

British captain George Dixon first circumnavigated Haida Gwaii. He then traded for otter pelts at the village of Sgan Gwaii. (Today, this spot harbors a mystical cluster of leaning, weathered totem poles, constituting a United Nations World Heritage Site commonly called Ninstints.) Soon thereafter, American captain John Kendrick showed up drunk and careless, let the Haida pilfer his laundry and seize his ship, then massacred them in return.

(Curiously, American connections also accompanied the recent Haida art renaissance with Bill Reid [son of an American father/Haida mother] and Robert Davidson [born in America/raised on Haida Gwaii] at the forefront. Canadian twenty-dollar bills now display a Reid carving with Haida figures mimicking "George Washington crossing the Delaware." Perhaps brash and reserved cultures mix like oil and vinegar but produce tasteful blends of artistic sensitivity and marketing chutzpah.)

Once the white folk actually moved into the neighborhood, intercultural relations went from bad to about the same. The primary Haida social institution was the potlatch: a massive, extended feast on the scale of Rio's Carnival—masks, music, dancing, dining, visions, ceremonies, plus redistribution of wealth by gift-giving. The introduction of European goods cranked up the volume on the whole affair.

Consequently, British Columbian politicians had to outlaw potlatches. Why? Well, communal property, ecstatic visions, beads and feathers—white people wouldn't be allowed to act like that till the 1960s. Besides, all that reckless spending, elder competition, glitz and greed—it almost stole the spotlight from the soon-to-be-invented provincial lottery. In short, the prohibition was arbitrary.

Before long, missionaries decided that totem poles were also evil. Not understanding their function as official record and coat-of-arms, they assumed them to be a competitive brand of deity. Some clergy-types even abandoned the free and open exchange of ideas for kerosene and a match.

The Haida were thus stripped of their organization and their database, but the deadliest blow of all had already been dealt invisibly. The smallpox virus passed silently from one European with acquired immunity to one aboriginal without protection. In that unrecorded, unintended moment, ninety-percent of the Haida were condemned to die.

We moderns congratulate ourselves too often on how tolerantly we'd have handled such a culture clash. Talk is cheap. The Haida no longer constitute a perceived threat and no ship logs document our anxiety about driving an RV into Nicaragua or our anger at a Malaysian cop requesting a tip/bribe.

Staring into the gray abyss around the ship, I certainly had no eagerness to meet a large, armed group of trans-nationals with a different conduct code and language. I love adventure, but the occasional lighthouse or coastguard beam is okay too. Much has changed since the bad old days, but perhaps our world is not really more enlightened, just better lit.

Finally, along came Buck. After growing up a pampered pet in the California sunshine, this St. Bernard/Scottish Shepherd was kidnapped then sold as a sled dog. He, too, passed shipboard through Hecate Strait, en route to the Klondike gold rush. In this northern wilderness, he learned both the beauty of nature and the law of club and fang.

Yes, Buck is a fictional character from Jack London's *Call of the Wild*. However, he's more. He's the biography of so many who've grown up domesticated and urbanized, only to find their spirit-home in the purity and vitality of wilderness. That's what brought me to Haida Gwaii: the longing for my primal self, my totem spirit, if you will.

Eventually, our ship docked and I stepped aground. Finding myself in a circle of elders, I joined a discussion of that day's *Vancouver Sun* headline: "Salmon Runs Disastrously Low." We also stared at clear-cut logging scars—at best, nature with a bad haircut, at worst, an eco crime scene.

By dark, I was sitting alone, next to a crackling fire on a bluff overlooking a beach. All night I sat, dozing then dreaming then waking then reflecting.

Just before dawn, I saw him: a barefoot warrior with conical spruce hat, grizzly-bear-tattooed chest, and mother-of-pearl-studded cape. Flitting circuitously through the trees, he came up behind me. His left hand held out a Hudson's Bay blanket; his right index finger jabbed my attention to a particular spot. "I don't see anything," I protested.

He stared back without emotion, "Neither did we." A smallpox plague spread by infected trade blankets … who could've foreseen it?

Sunrise woke me. I gazed out over the islands of Haida Gwaii and the surrounding sea—sacred ground and holy water for old and new reasons. These shores, framed by Alaska and mainland British Columbia, constitute spawning ground for much of our world's remaining wild salmon. While indigenous people have always revered this super-protein wonder-fish, the general public has only recently grasped that farmed salmon are no substitute for dwindling wild stocks. Of course, before the Haida could defend these stocks from extinction they had to do the same for themselves.

Now, rising from the ashes, the Haida again defend their sacred ground and holy water. With today's war canoes pointed at oil rigs and fish farms, a long-silenced drumbeat steadily rises. Is it melodramatic to lump this current environmental spat with the Haida's ancient struggle to survive? Maybe. After all, white man's science has not yet proven that oil drilling and fish farming will significantly harm this fragile ecosystem. Perhaps we should give them a try … as long as there are no blankets involved.

After wolfing down breakfast, I rejoined the elders. Their circle soon became a medicine wheel. A longhaired shaman mixed tobacco, cedar, fungi, and leaves in an abalone shell bowl. He then lit the concoction. As it smoldered, aromatic wisps rose in phantasmal helixes. Waving an eagle feather over each of us in turn, this "skaggy" administered a baptism by smoke.

Shallow buckskin drums took up a fast, thunder-like rhythm. Whistles and chants burst from otherwise stoical faces. Frenzied dancers emerged, wearing masks that transformed them into mythic beings from killer whales to cannibals. Physical and spiritual dimensions were merged in ways I couldn't fully understand. What I did see clearly was that my culture has abandoned both superstition of and connection with nature. In embracing a scientific worldview, we've lost our instinctual mystic vision.

As a pipe passed around, prayers were offered to the Creator. They acknowledged four directions: North, South, East, and West, with four elements: earth, wind, fire, and water, then four colors: red, yellow, black, and white, symbolizing four peoples: Americans, Asians, Africans, and Europeans. The circle concluded with the pronouncement: "Everything is related."

We feasted to celebrate the fall equinox then retired to a sweat lodge. The elders told me that a pipe stem represents man, a pipe bowl represents woman, and a sweat lodge represents the womb of life. (So, I wondered, what the hell were we doin' suckin' on the pipe stem?)

The sweat lodge seemed more tomb than womb. Searing hot rocks were piled in the center using antler tongs. Then the door closed, trapping us in crypt-like darkness. Even after focusing, my eyes saw nothing but the faint glow of these "grandfather stones." The shaman sprinkled them with herbs, emitting sparks, pops, and a scent palette ranging from wild celery to marijuana. Finally he doused them with water, flooding the air with suffocating heat.

For an unbearable two hours, I sat, struggling against drowning, fainting, and an ever-rising heart rate. It was crazy, but we all have our cherished quasi-virtues and "death before dishonor" is mine. When the door, at last, opened, it was only to insert more rocks. Yet, for a brief moment, I was a prisoner allowed a window, a diver reaching the surface, just until light, air, and hope were again mercilessly snuffed.

For another two hours, we gasped, howled, drummed, and prayed. On the last round, I deliriously tallied the number of voices yet to supplicate. I concluded I could make it without passing out, if the skaggy didn't go again at the end. He did. Damn that prayer hog!

Final conscious reflections: ancient man slept in dark caves, my ancestors homesteaded dark forests, I can barely survive this dark super-sauna, most of my peers can't stand a dark evening without TV. Yet, all of us, alike, are herded into that ultimate dark hole, from which there is no escape, which humanity's earliest writings call "sheol"—the grave.

Praying ceased. The door opened. I prepared to dive for that shining portal, but had to wait my turn, like the last varmint out of a hole. My turn never came.

I came to, five feet outside the door with everyone standing over me. Slimy grime covered my skin. Grimy slime came from my nose—a swollen, blood-trickling nose. Must have fallen on my face (literally and figuratively). All dignity abandoned, I searched my arm for less-muddy places to wipe pinkish snot in front of near strangers.

Someone handed me a half-peeled orange, in which I buried my face and my pride. Someone else told me that those who endure the sweat lodge till blacking out are considered heroic. I wasn't buying it. My body had refused to support my pretensions to immortality. In the game of Haida-and-seek, I was the first man out.

I returned home a disappointed alpha male. I'd seen no macho totem, no grizzly or wolf spirit—possibly because these species no longer inhabit the islands. Dreaming in my toasty bed, cool Haida forest transformed into hot delta bayou. Suddenly, I heard a low, mournful cry. It was Howlin' Wolf—not A howlin' wolf, THE Howlin' Wolf. You know, the blues singer.

Serves me right. Goofy white boy seeking a native vision up North sees a black man from down South. Alas, his message was incomprehensible and his verb conjugation was deplorable. Howlin' Wolf looked over and mumbled, "Boy, let me teach you theology: God be God … and you don't be."

Nearing the End of the World

Heaven and hell are best reached by paddle and sail. Thus, I am at sea. Heaven has shifted from afternoon blue to sunset red, from cauliflower cumulus to impressionistic cirrus. Gulls relinquish the faded sky. Diamond-white Venus in elongation burns for rust-ochre Mars in opposition, while a pounding, sloshing oceanic groove underscores the celestial lust. A new-moon sliver rises. Equatorial hunter Orion stalks the polar bear cub as darkness overtakes my longitude then my world.

The netherworld is also here. Around earth's metallic core, molten-rock magma constantly rises in searing-hot globules, through abundant cracks in the eggshell crust. Seems terra firma is more humpty dumpty. This Pacific Rim is especially just what it's cracked-up to be: a ring of fire hosting two-thirds of the world's volcanoes and most of its earthquakes. I'm on the seaway to hell. Yet, the inferno below fuels a wonder above, the Queen Charlotte Archipelago, to which I'm swooshing on a salty breeze.

My Captain-Cookish voyage has replaced gelatinous pork and scurvy with Dungeness crab and Chablis. Mine is a civilized pilgrimage. Still, I'm wearing boots, I didn't bring a razor, and I'm hoping to feel rugged or dangerous. Men have needs, you know. Like the wind, my citified heart is migrating from a high to a low-pressure zone; like the mainsail, my chest is burgeoning under a vast noctilucent expanse. I breathe in as if I just installed an extra lung.

Sunrise turns a starboard sea into a blinding nova and reveals a portside Orca pod—my morning epiphany. Our narrow-beam, long-hulled craft pushes twelve knots on GPS and coffee, while these matriarchal nuns with fins whiz by on sonar and salmon-breath. Herman Melville's Captain Ahab seizes my body, mumbling, "Aye ye damn-ed whales: curs-ed scourge of the deep!" I don't know what came over me—nautical road-rage, perhaps?

Near Port Hardy, we cross an immense darkened patch. Submerged kelp-trees perform synchronic ballet in rubbery amber tights. I stare down dreamily. Such undersea forests rival giant redwoods in height. (However, they suck for camping.) Suddenly, my eyes lock with those of an old man sporting a slick bald head, flared bulbous nose, and bushy gray mustache: a sea otter. One blink and he's gone.

Sea otters are the dominant predator of the tidal zone. Plus, their custom of whacking shellfish with rocks makes them the only nonprimate to use tools. They are voracious. Backstroking the thin line between killer whales and lethal humans, these swimming weasels munch on spiny red urchins and everything else that eats kelp. Their food-chain niche is irreplaceable. Without them, undersea forests are clear-cut and many coastal species cease to spawn. Hunted to virtual extinction, their pelts brought people Northwest. Multiplying in recent years, their recovery may allow us to stay.

Cruising mid British Columbia, one almost experiences a monotony of beauty. Coast, forest, mountains; coast, forest, mountains; headland, fjord; headland, fjord. The dawn bird-chorus repeats, "This is my territory. I'm still here, seeking single drab female to share accommodations." Babes of bird-dom are apparently near deaf. Eagles circle all day with effortless grace, riding ground thermals and negotiating landmarks. Geese pass over all night with migratory precision, aerodynamically configured and astronomically led.

Like the bald raptor, I've always looked more for earthly opportunities than heavenly guides. As Salman Rushdie's sighing Moor said, "We look up and hope the stars look down, we pray there may be stars for us to follow, moving across the heavens and leading us to our destiny, but it's only our vanity. We look at the galaxy and fall in love, but the universe cares less about us than we do about it. Our fates are here on earth. There are no guiding stars." Like Marcel Pagnol's Jean de Florette, "I could blame the heavens … but I'd rather take responsibility for my fate."

Nevertheless, tides crashing around me confirm there are irresistible forces of nature—even heavenly ones. If I'm such a cerebral, autonomous being, how come half my opinions change every time I make love? No, I'm part of creation: a creature. All plants photosynthesize ground minerals, sun fire, air carbon, and water hydrogen into carbohydrates. All animals live off these. Jean de Florette inherited ground but perished without water; the Moor had inner fire but collapsed without air. People who revere elemental forces aren't primitives, they're realists. The rest of us suffer delusions of grandeur. Captain Cook forgot this, until he was trapped between high ground and open water, where pacific islanders gave him a basic-elements-refresher-course in air gasping and fire roasting.

We pass alongside Princess Royal Island. This humanly uninhabited, virtually impenetrable Eden holds the last handful of white kermode bears. "Give us mutants!" my camera screams. "Enough pristine wilderness; we demand genetic abnormalities!" I chime in. Like her winged daughters, Mother Nature turns a mighty-attractive-but-deaf ear. I grudgingly submit myself to fate/providence. (Do the powers-that-be be or not be? That is the question!) A once-in-a-lifetime chance fades off into the distance with our shimmering, rippling wake.

Maturity somewhat lacking, I sulk long and hard over Ursus Invisibilus. Nature proffers more botanical perfection for appeasement, but I snub it like a cheap supermarket bouquet. My white-bears-only-need-apply attitude borders on eco-racism. Waaaaah! A ship horn finally ends my broodings as we dock in the Queen Charlotte Islands.

You may well wonder why the archipelago was thus named. The monarchic moniker was to establish British sovereignty. Ironically, Queen Charlotte wasn't British. She was German but married to England's King George III—the one who sent Captain Cook to the ends of the earth. However, George was equally German plus touched in the head and convinced that maidservants shouldn't mind being touched everywhere else. He was imported to avoid a Catholic on the throne. (Surely, the reader can grasp why an insane, lecherous German King of England would be better than a Catholic.)

So, that was Queen Charlotte and these are her remote wilderness islands on the far side of the world, which she never visited. Just as the King George III Islands have reverted to their traditional name (Tahiti), the Queen Charlottes are often called by the ancient title: Haida Gwaii, meaning land of the Haida people.

We tie up at a pier worth remembering. The clean, stocky government-maintained structure almost dares nature to erode it faster than the regularly scheduled upkeep. My boots clomp across firm planks and echo on crisp air. The gargantuan L-shaped platform offers a dizzying panorama shared only by chubby birds with proprietary egos. Of course, this is but half the pier. My eyes follow barnacle trails down to the ebony waterline, where unseen eyes doubtless look up in similar bewilderment at an equally unknown dimension. I hobble and wobble ashore.

Thousands of bright silver salmon and I arrive on the same dreary autumn day. We're all pretty thrashed by our journeys. However, I've no spawning to look forward to, so I lay down and die on a guesthouse mattress that only feels like a rocky streambed. (Doubtless, my host could retort that I only smell like a lovely fish.) This is the time of an annual Coho Derby, sponsored by the Sandspit Rod and Gun Club.

My snooze will be short. Set to join the angling, I'm up at the smack of dawn, wondering what hit me.

It starts with a pancake breakfast, as all things should. Alex, a likable local character, offers to take me fishing. We shatter the glassy surface of Hecate Strait with his EvinRude OMC 225. Our bow slams up and down, making each wave one small step for fishermen, one big thud for my behind. We're spanking the sea-god Neptune, which will surely come to no good.

Alex does a sudden death-defying circle around a terrified bird struggling to get aloft. "Do you see the loon? Do you see the loon?" he hollers maniacally.

"I see two loons," is my reply.

We eventually idle on a breathtaking seascape—slate gray sky, eggshell gray cloud, bluish gray land, metallic gray ocean, and a basic gray whale. This is a life moment I could never recapture. We're headed down the coastline toward Gwaii Haanas, which means "place of wonder." Rugged pristine islands, wild teeming fisheries, mystical Haida villages—a recent issue of *National Geographic Traveler* ranked it the best national park in all North America.

Scenery notwithstanding, Alex is a man on a mission. He fits Penn reels onto Shakespeare Ugly Sticks, attaches Apex Crippled Herrings plus anchovy bait, engages Scotty downriggers and trolls with a gleam in his eye. We see nothing for hours but cormorants. Recurring rain silts the water, dampens the spirit, and leaves the bait unnibbled. Our ocean-floor pictograph is as flat and featureless as the afternoon, except for one lone critter that blips the fish-finder then vanishes. Alex turns on station KCKN from Ketchikan, Alaska. The music and the motor thus compete for volume and, sometimes, artistic merit.

Finally, the big one strikes. Seizing a rod in each hand while vacillating between gloom and euphoria, Alex epitomizes Bipolar Fishing Syndrome. The salmon, which he hereafter refers to as "the prize contender," gets away. Alex now despairs of winning the derby. Yet, he has no intention of going home till he does. I stay alert, lest he run out of bait and try to cut a strip off me.

Luck turns with the tide. A pink mackerel, picking on someone his own size when biting the anchovy, comes first; a six-pound, speckle-tailed Spring comes next; an eleven-pound, black-tailed Coho comes last. As always, grabbing flopping fish is like catching cold, slimy, popping corn that looks at you accusingly. While we read the scale, our radio blares out, "He ain't heavy, he's my brother!" Some places, these fish might be mounted not discounted, but Alex dejectedly pulls up the lines as darkness falls. A massive school instantly crosses the monitor screen, adding insult to injury.

Back at the weigh-in, fish tales abound and expand. Most that got away could be described with two words: Moby Dick. Arguers debate over who's the best fisherman, while grumblers focus on the day's drizzly weather and the glory days' better catches. I interview a three-foot-tall angler with blond curls:

"Did you enjoy the fishing?"

"Ohhh Yeaaah!"

"What made the day so special?"

"God did!"

"Did it rain much?"

"Mostly on my tongue!"

"Think you'll catch a bigger one next year?"

"Maybe, but I'll be way bigger!"

Who's the best fisherman? That's one thing about this "place of wonder" that inspires no wonderment at all. Our young heroine fished with childlike gratitude; we fished with childish attitude. Hemingway's aged hero fished with noble stoicism; we fished with banal obsession. I resolve to likewise become "way bigger" and compose no more chapters of "The Old Fart and The Sea."

Daybreak commences with birds. Not exotic birds, but plain brown starlings with tiny white spots that turn into patches when ruffled, just like I could see back home, not soaring across the firmament, but digging worms on the guesthouse lawn. Why do I notice them? Because there are more, more in a few meters than I've ever seen in an entire urban park. Sensing my presence at the window, they flee. So numerous, they sound like horses' hooves; so choreographed, they seem to share a brain. Maybe Alfred Hitchcock was on to something.

Today I meet Neil Carey, the nautical man's nautical man. His house is easy to find but hard to see. The property is piled high with beach combings—glass, plastic, Styrofoam, everything that floats and drifts ashore—all categorized with stenciled signs. (Why have yard sales when you can have a yard museum?)

The eighty-four-year-old stands erect in his cozy den, next to a whale jawbone under a life-ring bearing the name of Captain Ahab's ship, Pequod. We rehearse his Navy career from 1940 to 1965 and from Sailor to Lieutenant Commander. We discuss his stints aboard Norwegian whaling vessels. We relive his homesteading in the remote anchorage of Puffin Cove on the Charlotte's wild west coast from 1967 to 1993. I am in awe.

Lest the reader suppose me to have lost all objectivity, I freely admit there are greater seafarers than Neil Carey—for example, his wife. In 1937, Betty paddled a dugout canoe over 1,000 miles from Anacortes, Washington up the inside passage to Ketchikan, Alaska. (No, that isn't a misprint.) After this feat, she bore two loving sons, bore with a military husband for sixty-four winters, and before me sits with ninety-one summers of sparkle in her eye. As I photograph her with the famous canoe, she blushes, "This is a little embarrassing. I look so old."

Surgically contorted Desperate Housewives, as eager to be filmed as to bang the plumber, pass before my eyes like red before a bull. "Betty," I blurt out, "You look elderly, but you look radiant and God help the civilization that doesn't want your picture!" Now, I admit: I've lost all objectivity. Beauty can do that to you. I depart with very moist eyes as two ancient mariners hold a steady course to the setting sun and wave from behind a pile of seashells.

Wanting to get out of touch with my sensitive side, I hit the local nightspot for beer and hot wings—food you can grip with your hands, tear with your teeth, and wipe with your sleeve. Chris, the waitress, both staves and stokes my appetite. Olympic-gold hair-ringlets crown her curvaceously muscled body, which is squeezed into white jeans and draped in sleeveless purple satin with lace. She writes gothic horror and is the kind of girl who could make punishment and reward synonymous.

Laughing out loud on my left is redheaded Dawn-Ann. The freckles on her creamy shoulders call out to be included among the known constellations. She's the kind of girl you'd ask out even if you hadn't been drinking, except that her boyfriend mans the coast guard unit controlling all routes off the island. She generously loans me a Jeep Cherokee to drive around during my stay.

Nodding-off to my right is raven-haired Brenna. The dimples on her copper cheeks ensure I'll never look at pit mines the same way again. She invites me to go kayaking and is the kind of girl you'd paddle with even if you had a burning rash below the waterline. We agree on a morning rendezvous.

Across the room, a dartboard league (yes, there is such a thing) warms up for weekly competition. Seniors and loggers form a line—bald spots next to baseball caps, needles raised at targets like junkies driving home hypodermics. Behold the Mount Olympus of pub games. Silly? Yes, but no more so than our geeky writer poising and thrusting his pen with equal fervor.

Stumbling home in darkness along the crescent shoreline, my senses compensate for lost vision. I can't see that it's low tide, but hear that it's distant tide; I can't see roadside houses, but smell cedar-wood fires; I can't see the guesthouse driveway but feel the familiar gravel. I know not whether this bawdy night's account be entirely credible, but let the magic of beer, my happy-hoppy muse, spill over onto the reader who canst now view life through the pint-size looking glass and still operate heavy machinery.

Brenna and her companions—Bianca, Civa, and Luc—turn out to be quite the adventurers. The expedition itinerary includes: drive to Moresby Camp; take a zodiac into Gwaii Haanas to Hotspring Island; savor the elemental Jacuzzi of subterranean fire, concaved earth, mineralized water, and chilled air; camp overnight; recover a stash of kayaks, coffee, smoked salmon, and venison; paddle through Juan Perez Sound to Bischoff Island then on to Sac Bay; camp another night; trek up the island's spine to a colossal unnamed lake; cross three ridges, two waterfalls, much unstable moss, and no trails; descend to the Pacific through gathering darkness, dense shrubbery, slippery roots, flowing mud, and sucking bogs; sleep in Neil Carey's leaky cabin on Puffin Cove; backtrack home.

I wouldn't recommend the experience—unless you like vast horizons strewn with islets, tidal pools strewn with shellfish, deserted beaches strewn with driftwood, and primeval forests strewn with nothing human at all.

On my last day before leaving Haida Gwaii, I set out to visit some of the many artists who live and draw inspiration here. Must first get to Graham Island. A recorded government phone-message says the Alliford Bay ferry departs for Skidegate at 9:00 a.m. I jump in the Jeep, barrel past photo ops as if they're outhouses, and arrive at 8:58 a.m. No cars, no people, no ferry. The weathered government sign contradictingly insists: "Year-Round Schedule—Leave

Alliford Bay 9:30 a.m." The tide laps metrically, a raven caws occasionally, 9:30 passes uneventfully.

I now spot a temporary sign: "BC Ferries Appreciates Your Patience As We Provide Alternate Service." Alternate? What does that mean? More? Less? Better? Worse? Gay? Straight? I've no idea. Only one thing is clear: BC Ferries appreciates patience. If I had some spray-paint, the sign might also read: "Lyn appreciates information." At precisely 10 o'clock, a raven flies low overhead with a hwoom-hwoom-hwoom helicopter-like whipping sound and the ferry arrives.

In Queen Charlotte City, I brunch with well-known carver and Haida Nation President Ghindigin Howasti Guujaaw at Queen Bee's Coffee House. We sip mocha amidst Ganesha silks, Buddha masks, Persian rugs, Victorian lamps, cedar boughs, bovine skulls, rainbow geckos, bamboo partitions, leopard-print cushions, jade chess sets, and iridescent flower paintings by local artist Kiki van der Heiden.

This seems an odd way to spend Thanksgiving. Yet, a pilgrim in a new land sharing table with a Native chieftain isn't entirely without precedent. Besides, gourds and field corn are so overrated. Our multicultural feast includes indigenous cacao plus elegant mass-produced mugs courtesy of paleface Henry Ford and Pequod first mate Starbuck.

Guujaaw seems a most honorable man who dotes tenderly over his sweet daughter Xiila. I'm also supposed to say a wonderful time of mutual exchange and understanding is had by all. However, I'm a nonfiction writer. My heart wants to be pals, but my brain detects our social cogwheels are differently calibrated and grind a little when pressed together.

While planning this trip by phone, I noted Sandspit Caucasians responding to questions about Skidegate events with "You'll have to talk to *them* about that," and Skidegate Natives answering similar inquiries about Sandspit doings with "You'll have to talk to *them* about that." Birds of a feather still often flock together. Whether we do this because we're racists or just because shared mores simplify life isn't always clear. Perhaps in some better world—some newer-than-Columbus's-or-Colin-Farrell's new world—we'll all break bread together. Hopefully, Martin Luther King has already fired-up the barbeque.

Driving through Skidegate, I pass grand, fierce totem poles and a beachfront Haida-language school. In the hamlet of Tlell, site of the yearly Edge of the World Music Festival, I stop at Dress For Less. This eclectic eatery purveys vintage clothes, lavender massage oils, and marijuana-leaf-covered journals.

Proprietor Leslie serves up food in a Scottish kilt under signage reading: "All unattended children will be given two shots of espresso and a free puppy." She offers me vegan or meat chili and cornbread. I've got no problem with meat but do insist on further identification. This is buffalo and, mmm-mmm, it did not die in vain.

Fellow-diner Dan just finished high school in Golden and is hitchhiking across the province. He elaborates, "Hitchhiking has honed my instincts. It's forced me to follow my hunches, trust in coincidences, and take chances. It's a glorious paradox of rolling the dice and manifesting my destiny." Well said. Everything else he says, over his vegan chili, smacks of B-vitamin deficiency.

Continuing North, I reach the Tlell River, home of Steelhead trout and artist James Houston. His red-roofed, green-doored, fly-rod-adorned cabin perches idyllically over the winding estuary. Here, this three-time-winner of the Canadian Library Association Book of the Year Award wrote *Hideaway: Life on the Queen Charlotte Islands*. Here, this master glass designer envisioned his seventy-foot-high central sculpture for the Glenbow-Alberta Art Museum and smaller sculpture for the King of Saudi Arabia. Yet, here, he is not. Jim and his wife Alice winter in New England. Therefore, I keep driving.

En route to Port Clements, the view is tree-farm replants and black-tail deer. Just past a logging-machinery museum, I ask directions at the Yakoun River Pub—empty except for three women with about six teeth and nine shots of whisky. Frighteningly friendly overtures hasten me along to Massett.

Evelyn van der Hoop warmly welcomes me into her kitchen that overlooks shining Massett Inlet. She's an accomplished Haida weaver. After completing her degree in art and psychology, she worked in Martha's Vineyard, where Jackie Onassis once hung one of her creations at home. In May 2000, she was Artist in Residence at the Smithsonian. This year her work appears in the Vancouver Art Gallery's exhibition, "Raven Traveling: Two Centuries of Haida Art." Now, she fetches from the bedroom a newly finished wool-and-cedar-bark ceremonial costume. The blue and yellow palette is rich and vibrant. I'm thrilled to snap the first-ever photo of this masterpiece.

Though the garment respectfully honors traditional protocol, something has changed. As culture secularizes, so do objects. Her craft has evolved from a thing of mystic power to one of largely artistic potency. (They say art galleries are churches for humanists.) Still, the dichotomy may be exaggerated. Haida Gwaii is a place where the natural and supernatural easily blur, where accepting the normal often means embracing the magical, where ecology and theology mostly overlap.

I take a detour to gaze down North Beach toward Rose Spit. In Haida mythology, this peninsula is where prankster/creator Raven coaxed male humans out of the razor clamshell (a mollusk with phallic-looking muscle) and mated them with red chitons (a mollusk with vagina-looking underside) to birth humanity in "the calm following the storm." Beyond Rose Spit lies Hecate Straight, named for Greek mythology's goddess guarding the isles at the western end of the world. This is the northern end of my world, the farthest I've been.

Heading back, I burn rubber. How shall I say this delicately? Though the bison no longer thunder across the high plain, at least one is stampeding through the lower intestine. Stop at my quaint guesthouse home to let the buffalo roam and pick up luggage. Drop off the Jeep and start walking for the airport.

Little do I know I'm about to meet one more artist. Wood, canvas, glass, and wool, are now joined by earth-mixed-with-water-baked-in-fire-and-cooled-by-air. As rain begins pouring, a luxury SUV gives me a ride. The driver is renowned tile crafter Sid Dickens. This Emily Carr College of Art and Design alumnus is a collector of dramatic historical relics and the developer of world-famous "Memory Blocks." We chat briefly, bypass his sprawling candlelit manse flanked by gardens and ponies, then part ways at the terminal.

Neil and Betty Carey show up to get me all weepy before I have to look calm and composed for the strip-search/X-ray guy. (Forget racial profiling; keep those sweet little grandparents out of high security areas!) My Air Canada Bombardier Dash 8 is soon rising high above the islands.

To Haida, this is the place of origin. To me, it's the end of the world. Our world officially lost its geographical and psychological edges after Columbus. For well-rounded global-community-lovers, that was a good thing, but for us romantic loners, not so much.

We modern explorers often discover that the known world really is a bit flat. Like Allie Fox on the Mosquito Coast or Bruce Chatwin in Patagonia, we need the end of the earth to be a place, not just a frame of mind. Along with Herman Melville's Ishmael, we're "tormented by an everlasting itch for things remote." This obsession is elusive as any whale, despite we throngs of travel writers occupying the lofty mastheads of literary vessels and shouting, "Thar she blows!"

Today's spacecraft are named after Captain Cook's ships because paddle and sail no longer transport "farther than any man has gone before." Yet they can still take anyone farther than he or she has gone before. Maybe that's enough.

As I levitate through cloudbank wrapping the islands like a warm Haida blanket, my heart remains far below, breaking with the endless opalescent tides. Poor Queen Charlotte, she doesn't know what she missed.

Dying With Dignity Mexican Style

For Whom the Bowl Flushes

My life in Mexico began with the cockroach incident. First morning in my new home, a toilet wouldn't flush and a rising desert sun promised to bake the unsavory contents. I stepped into the shower.

Shampoo had just covered my closed eyes when I felt the tile floor move. One eye cocked open. An antennae-waving mega-roach scurried frantically around my feet. I yelled. I danced. We were trapped together like Aztec prisoners in a stone ball court. As he darted up my leg, I jerked, flinging him into the nearby fecal stew.

Several deep breaths stopped my trembling. La cucaracha paddled desperately through putrid seas while I stood above in godlike indifference to his plight. His fate was not so special. For many, life is crappy and then you die. I came to Queretaro for such existential reflection, but first, I needed a plunger.

Took a taxi across town. Decals of the grim reaper and a laughing skull adorned my side of the windshield. Conversation pieces perhaps? Or maybe, while other cabs post assurances of the driver's safety record, Mexican taxis prefer to remind us that death comes to us all in our own time; thus the beer-scented chauffer furiously street racing his amigos has nothing to do with it.

Ah, the philosopher/cabby. Stickers of Catholic saints nearly blocking out his field of vision offered further proof of his enlightened (if impeded) view. Now that's faith! Plus, the white-knuckled passenger received a potent evangelistic pitch to make peace with his maker.

I disembarked at Jardin Zenea. Children strolled with ice cream cones and couples kissed with uninhibited passion. Church bells clanged. The sound emanated from a stonework dome towering over the ochre-plastered Templo de San Francisco which was founded in the 1500s as a convent. I descended into the dark interior. A gory life-sized crucifix forced me left where flickering candlelight revealed a chapel and an imposing glass crypt dominated the scene. Inside, an orange-haired green-faced Jesus bled profusely onto his white-cotton death shroud, looking much like a reject from a bad CSI set. Revulsion outweighed inspiration.

Mexicans have an obsession with death that tends to mystify and mortify gringos. Yet, could it be our culture's ritual denial that is truly bizarre? I was determined to wallow in the macabre with my brown brethren to find out. A policeman posted just outside the cathedral with pistol, automatic rifle, and ammunition strap reiterated that death is a fact of life that locals make no effort to conceal.

A Cock & Bull Story

Friday was National Independence Day. My death pilgrimage led me to the corrida de toros or charging of the bulls. Hemingway loved such bullfights for the romance. I was here because the sun also sets and in Mexico it often sets blood red.

The crowd was mildly inebriated. We sat on brick risers between a dusty arena and a misty waterfall. Flamenco guitar filled the air. A black bull hurled itself into the walls as sleek men in gilded pastel costumes tormented it from all sides. Snack vendors combed the aisles.

A blindfolded and padded horse served as victim for the bull's furious goring to facilitate its rider grinding a spear into the bull's neck. (This wound forces the animal to charge head downward and horns forward.) A thick magenta mantle oozed over taurine torso and coagulated on a yellow prize ribbon. Mothers chatted with babysitters via cellphone. The beast took on a glazed stare as bloody slather dripped from its lifeless leathery tongue. Matador Fernando Ochoa stepped out to roaring applause.

El toro and el matador (which means killer) danced a swirling ballet. With each turn, horns and bulk passed within inches of the machismo artiste who skillfully hypnotized a mountain of testosterone into a delirious death cadence. The romance was highly questionable, but the finesse was indisputable.

The famous red cape conceals a silver sword. Fernando brandished it like a crosshair between raging eyes and snorting nostrils a yard away. (The fatal stab must be timed when hooves are together thus splaying shoulder blades.) Silence—the lunge, the strike, the collapse. This creature, born to hulking domination, crumbled finally into breathless submission. El toro had left the building. A pathetic bag of bones was dragged away with little dignity or notice.

Torrential rain swept in. The drag marks became a long purple puddle and the arena floor became a terra cotta swamp. A yellow bull stormed out with a raspy roar. Attacking his tormentors, he lost footing, crashed into a barrier, and broke off half a horn. His sound and fury signifying nothing, he now appeared an inelegant adversary and was soon replaced by a 600 kilogram, reddish, bellowing streak of anger that nearly hurdled the wall on entrance.

Matador Rafael Ortega took off his shoes for mud traction. Time after time, slip after slide, his lance missed the mark, turning all efforts to end the misery into meatball surgery. Japanese executives in cowboy hats clapped as if this was a new twist on Teppan-Yaki. The bullring became a lake. Rafael and apprentices retreated to high ground, where they discussed the logistical nightmare; elite patrons retreated to shelter, where they bemoaned the damp inconvenience. Across still-rising waters, a solitary bovine clump occasionally twitched.

Were this Transylvania, the night's bloodlust would likely have been satisfied. However, this was Mexico. Our movable fiesta migrated to the crumbling stone bowels of an old Franciscan mission for the torneo de gallos or cockfight. (Perhaps the Spaniards weren't such an obvious choice to "civilize" the indigenous peoples.) How do I characterize this cultural event? Picture 700 men, with 500 cigars, 300 tequila bottles, and 100 women of the sort who become sexually aroused by homicidal chickens.

Amidst the smoky drunken chaos, bets were placed two ways. Officials threw around a slotted tennis ball into which you crammed your wager; spectators shoved money in your face, which you were expected to match. Disputes were resolved quickly or violently.

The well-bred cocks were a lustrous green or red. Claws were accentuated with razor-sharp steel blades. Tournaments were a momentary flurry of screeches and feathers. Losers were often dead. When a bird survived, the owner orally sucked the blood from its throat to protect his investment. When both competitors were unresponsive, they were laid together and the winner (using the term loosely) was he whose beak hit the floor last. I'm not making this up!

Finding no thrill in animal cruelty, I was just about to leave when I noticed the curvaceous aficionado next to me licking her lips. "Well," I silly-gized, "if animals are going to suffer, mankind should receive some benefit." Not all the cocks that parried and thrust that night had feathers, and that's no worn-out, wet and dirty bull.

Bootylicious & Decomposing Bodies

The following weekend, I discovered Mexicans not only enjoy watching death, they like flirting with it as well. Drove to San Miguel de Allende. This picturesque pseudo-authentic town keeps its rustic charms with a combination of modern zoning laws, tourist cash flow, and quaint shops run by bohemian foreigners. The authentic Mexicans, of course, are mostly busy in non-authentic places hustling jobs to spare their children from quaint rustic poverty. In short, San Miguel is theater, a place where white folks find burros and sombreros while brown folks elsewhere seek carros and cappuccinos.

Today was slightly different. The main drag was packed with rich boys in white shirts and red bandannas (chico rico rancheros), putting on a good buzz and awaiting the release of the bulls. (I'm not saying that youth is wasted on the young; I'm simply noting that some youth were wasted on the street.)

When the terrified little cows finally came scampering down the cobblestone, it was about as glamorous as watching tipsy Mardi Gras revelers dodging parade floats. The bulls tried their best to avoid the staggering morons and were generally successful. "Bowling for drunks" pretty well sums it up.

My flirting-with-death reference had nothing to do with these bovine/hooligan antics. The real danger was in the crowd. Each tiny side street held a standing-by ambulance and about a thousand liquored-up fresas pressing against the barricade. (Fresa is Spanish for a strawberry or a girl who thinks shopping is the purpose of life.)

The strawberries and I were quickly becoming compote. As I was compressed from the front ambulance bumper to the door to the gas tank to the rear wheel, my will to live and my will to be smushed to death by beautiful women struck up an internal dialog. However, in the crucial moments, my duty to you the reader kept me alive.

Every few minutes, some unconscious person was passed back through the crowd. Without warning, an unsuccessful ambulance-climber above me sat on my head. She apologized, but this only confused me since it was pretty much the highlight of my day. I think I saw a bull running, but with my face plastered into the filthy window of an open rear ambulance door, it's difficult to say for sure. Next time I'll play it safe and run with the bulls.

With near death and animal death behind me, I felt prepared for something truly hard-core. Time for another road trip. My destination city of Guanajuato wasn't so much constructed as sculpted out of solid rock. From the subterranean labyrinth of stone tunnels, to the stone palaces of historic mining barons, to the stone streets, lampposts, walls, and bridges, this town was hewn to last.

Even mortal flesh lingers here. Guanajuato's ground minerals not only sustain the living, they preserve the dead. A bizarre sampling of pickled Homo sapiens has been warehoused to enlighten and disgust at the Mummy Museum. Thanks to many locals who can no longer afford grave rental for barely decomposing relatives, this establishment serves up a daily visual feast of peasant under glass.

I bought my ticket and swallowed hard. First came a black and white photo gallery where parents held deceased children. The poses were reserved, but the eyes burned with grief. Mothers looked stunned and distant; fathers seemed bursting with rage or crumbling with despair. A miner in a dirty suit cradled his sleeping princess in a white frilly dress. A circle of gaunt children tenderly supported their lost sibling's slumping head. This was life: the movie, not coming soon to a theatre near you.

Perhaps using dead children for spiritual education props and pay-per-view entertainment is inappropriate. If so, someone forgot to tell the Mexicans. One proprietor acknowledged the tackiness then pointed to hordes of foreign tourists quipping, "Which is worse: to sin for pay or to pay for sin?"—savvy museum official 1, sanctimonious journalist 0.

The threshold of the Mummy Museum proper passed beneath signage reading: "As you see me, so you shall be." A faint smell of musty rot offered further forewarning of things to come. Inside, the walls were stacked with glass vaults containing leathery remains that once walked and talked.

A sincere but incompetent friend strove to translate the tour narration. Our guide would speak for several minutes then my pal would say, "This is another mummy, he's dead," or "More mummies, they're dead too." I abandoned the tour de farce for the company of those who say nothing but communicate much.

Some corpses were organized in bone rows by human hands seeking meaning and order, but most had succumbed under nature's hand into varying degrees of chaos—clumps of hair, sagging flesh, loose fingernails, deflated lips, shriveled penises, dried-up eyeballs, broken-off toes, and peeling-off faces.

A skeleton in pleated shirt and silk waistcoat grimaced the word "Nooooo!" with enough terror to make Edward Munch's "The Scream" look like a Monet garden. One resident in cowboy boots held a note: "Simon Lozano, miner, died 1900, exhumed 1907." How ironic to spend your life in underground darkness and your death under floodlights.

I stood in absolute horror before a woman with dusty petrified labia, still-visible clitoris, tightly-clutched breasts, and head jerked back in an agonized scream suggesting that death and orgasm are nearly indistinguishable and the former may be more familiar to us than we wish to believe.

The mummies continued ad nauseum. A fetus showed an umbilical cord dried across a tiny chest. A baby in diaper and blue sweater with chubby rotting cheeks gripped a doll with its few remaining fingers. A blackened crispy elder retained beard, mustache, and pubic hairs. A pregnant woman bore heaps of collapsed belly skin and breasts like dehydrated figs.

The sickening parade ended and I finally emerged into sunlight. A street vendor extended arms loaded with toy mummies. I laughed in disbelief. "More mummies? More mummies? Do I want more mummies? Are you kidding?" I found a place to sit down and think about anything but mummies.

Christmas Greetings from the Inferno

The gringo/Latino death-perspective-gap can also be found traveling southeast from the Bajio. I arrived in Bernal one weekend along with swarms of tourists. The village had few services, dirt lot pay parking, and rental toilets with extra charge for paper. So, why was everyone there?—only one reason: Bernal has a rock. Granted, it's a big beautiful rock with a stunning view from the top, but it's still a rock. Hippies and retirees flock to the rock and its reputed life-sustaining aura, whatever that means. Mexican locals are quite content to turn their backs on the monolith to welcome tourists with their life-sustaining aura of cash.

Nearly all of these visitors come to the rock through the junction town of San Juan Del Rio. Very few stop at the straightforwardly-named "Museum of Death," though admission and parking are free. My tour group included only young Mexican couples on what some would consider an odd first date. Here you walk across many elegantly carved rocks with mystical symbols. However, these are burial headstones. Rather than offering a panoramic vista, they provide only a glimpse into the abyss. Our guide expounded passionately on displayed artwork portraying all manner of persons awaiting their appointment with death. While most gringos are vaguely conscious of this inevitability, when it comes to metaphysics, we prefer less talk more rock.

I returned to Queretaro on Sunday night to learn that even Christmas can't escape the kiss of death in Mexico. Though still early in the season, the main plaza had transformed into an elaborate twinkling Navidad display, divided into four quadrants. The first illustrated the star trek of wise men from the East; the second offered shepherds prostrate before the angelic messengers; the third glorified the baby in a barn lying in a manger. (Oh, don't give me that fashionable blank stare, you know the story, and as for you New York literary types, word search baby Jesus!)

With this totally unsecularized presentation, readers may wonder if the city fathers provided anything relevant to those of other faiths or none. Why yes, they did. The fourth quadrant portrayed a flaming hell with the damned in eternal death, surrounded by twelve-foot-tall nightmarish demons.

Now, if you're a little shaky on the connection between tidings of great joy and tidings of your-ass-is-grass, I'm with you. However, one needed only scan the beaming faces that packed the square to see that most locals were quite comfortable with a yuletide admonition of "joy to the world or else." Don't tell Bing Crosby, but not everyone is dreaming of a white man's Christmas.

Come Wednesday, death made another appearance on an even less expected occasion. Have you ever been to a children's birthday party where you felt like killing a couple of kids? Who hasn't? Yet, only in Mexico have I seen the deed actually done.

Preparations began six hours before celebration time. Two woolly bleating kids were tethered to a tree. Suddenly, one was seized, its legs bound with coarse biting rope. A knife was inserted by a neck jab you could feel—a shocked convulsive squirm, a dramatic sigh with a simultaneous expulsion of poop pellets, a mixture of drowning and breathing from the neck gash, a bucket filling with goopy cherry-red blood, a woozy docile resistance followed by unconscious reflexive resistance followed by stillness.

The sibling stood by waiting his turn as obliviously as most of us do. The bloody knife lay on the cream tile looking like a movie poster. When a stick was thrust up the lifeless hind leg, long-closed eyes horribly snapped open. Using this entryway, the carcass was blown up like a raft to separate the meat for butchery. The dead animal was then hung from a hook with the head dragging clunkily across the stones and a gaping white aorta dripping like PCP pipe.

The inflators spit the bad taste from their mouths while I wondered if I should do the same. Our sibling sensed something negative and preferred to face the other way. Don't we all? Behind patio-door glass, a three-year-old brown face was sobbing. I assumed she was weeping for the kid; turned out she was crying because she wanted to see. Perhaps aversion to death is learned, not inborn.

The distilled blood was cooked with chilies, onions, herbs, and green tomatoes to make taco filling. The flesh and bones were grilled over a pot of garbanzos, potatoes, carrots, and onions, resting on white hot coals in a stone pit. This was covered with maguey leaves, plywood, and finally a mound of dirt. Four hours later, the pile was shoveled off to reveal succulent meat and zesty consommé.

A long fiesta table was spread over the spot where the killing took place. Small burgundy stains under the chairs went unnoticed. The greazy broth, served with chopped onions and cilantro, was strong as goat gravy mixed with sheep bathwater. The solidified-blood tacos had virtually no flavor, for which I was truly grateful. Our sacrificial lambs even attained an afterlife in the many photos of guests gnawing bones. A fly-covered bucket of hooves and organs, abandoned off to one side, comprised the final frame in my memory—a birthday, a deathday, a normal Mexican day.

Gettin' Drunk with Dead Relatives

Why are Mexicans so unusually comfortable with death? One possible reason is that they are less likely to die alone or forgotten than their northern counterparts. Death, like everything else here, is a family affair.

On November 2nd, the Day of the Dead, I went with a friend's family to a little town called Pueblito, which means "little town." The cemetery was packed with crowds of people and rows of porta-potties. Carnival-like vendors sold fresh bouquets and chocolate skulls. We negotiated the maze of above-ground cement rectangles, some of which were being lovingly painted and others of which were serving as picnic tables, to their grandfather's plot. After arranging flowers and reciting rosaries, we sat on grandpa's grave to play guitar and drink pulque cactus beer. (The man resting beneath us had died trying to cross a desert on foot into the US. How dare he scorn the immigration laws made by esteemed men like Richard Nixon and Bill Clinton in order to feed his offspring? I guess he got what he deserved.)

In theory, Day of the Dead is to remind people that life must be lived with gusto and forebears should be remembered with gratitude. In practice, it's more like a tailgate party on a tomb. However, compared to Halloween, where we introduce children to the occult while jumpstarting their diabetes, this is good clean fun.

I for one would be happy to have my bone box used for dining furniture or an accordion concert, if it helps the next generation view life more as spiritual quest than shopping spree. (I would also be thrilled to have this writing constitute a legal will, if it reduces the global lawyer population by one. I would thus herein claim to be of sound mind and body, but those who've read my work or seen me naked could easily testify otherwise.)

Liked the Holocaust?

You'll love the Aztecs!

Another likely contributor to the Mesoamerican death fetish is the longstanding local tradition of brutality and slaughter. Regional history somewhat resembles the Mel Gibson flick. Plus, don't tell Mel, but the Mayans were sissies compared to the Aztecs.

One lazy afternoon, I stood inside the Pyramid of the Feathered Serpent Quetzalcoatl at Mexico City's Museum of Anthropology. Below me were skeletons of sacrificial victims wearing human jawbone necklaces—Mexico's answer to the Hawaiian lei. Spend a day in this world renowned art collection and you'll see clearly that the death cult has long been inseparable from Mesoamerican civilization.

Olmecs near Veracruz portrayed the death god well before 1000 BC. Half skull/half face shamanic masks along with evidence of ritual roasting, boiling, and defleshing cannibalism likewise survive from these early times. First Millennium citizens of Teotihuacán dubbed their main drag "The Avenue of the Dead" then mass produced gleaming obsidian blades and needle sharp skewers for daily executions. Early Second Millennium Toltec gave their reclining deity Chac Mool a belly bowl for stockpiling human hearts. (So much for those "wild fraternity ritual" stories.)

Just before closing time, I gawked at the famous Aztec Sun Stone, which celebrates the source of all life and currently adorns the ten-peso coin. Gringos like to pretend it's a calendar. Mexicans know it's a sacrificial altar. The center sun face has a knife tongue and holds two beating hearts. (Not so surprising from folks who roofed their buildings with skulls, covered every other flat surface with grinning death god motifs, and decapitated someone for each ball court foul … Even ratings starved NBA owners haven't tried this.) The sheer number of Aztec altars that have survived time ravaging and Spanish purging boggles the mind, without even noticing the built-in drain holes and trenches engineered to dispense with an ocean of blood. Need I go on? Suffice it to say: death themes are as common to Mexican heritage as corn.

Mesoamerican history loudly argues for the brevity and tragedy of existence rather than happily-ever-after Hollywood endings. So, to some extent, omnipresent mortality is a permanent fixture in Mexican psychology. There abides a Sun Tzu-like conviction that death is coeval with life and to prevail without resistance is best. Still, my experience suggests a deeper and more current explanation for why these people stare death squarely between the eyes.

With Mexican Chocolate, Who Needs Peyote?

While leaving Mexico, I had one more sobering brush with death—death by chocolate. The day was scorching hot. My vehicle had no air-conditioning. The more delirious I became the more determined I was to reach Zacatecas. Stopped for food and drink. The gas station had neither, except for the Mexican chocolate bars made entirely of cocoa, cinnamon, and sugar. I munched happily with no awareness of the dehydrating effects or of a fireball sunset magnifying through the rear window onto the back of my head.

Stuffed into a narrow canyon between craggy, arid mountains, Zacatecas often shimmers like a mirage. On that day, though, in my waterless sunstroked state, it positively wobbled back and forth and zoomed in and out. Near passing out, I negotiated a one-lane cobblestone alley with cars parked on both sidewalks toward a hotel shown on my map. Dead end.

Backing out was impossible and blacking out seemed inevitable. Could things get any worse? Suddenly, a street person, wearing an arm sling clearly concealing something other than an injury, stepped from the shadows and began urgently whistling for his accomplices. Putting a hand on my open window, he hissed that he'd help me if I'd just hand him the keys. I froze for an eternal second, wavering between fight and flight, until a police car lit up behind me. Ten minutes later, I stumbled into a Howard Johnson suite, threw up, and fell into bed.

The next morning as I loaded my suitcase, a passerby offered me three thousand US dollars to ride in my trunk, across two days of desert and over the border. Imagine. He was willing to pay dearly for a deadly ordeal that made mine look easy. Why? Because most Mexicans are all too aware of what we have in North America: economic wealth. However, little human cargo goes the other way, since most North Americans have no idea what treasures lie South of the Rio Grande.

Frankl-ly Speaking,
Kevorkian Don't Know Jack

Friedrich Nietzsche said that he who has a why to live can bear with almost any how. In concentration camps, Viktor Frankl confirmed this with his observation that those who saw purpose and meaning in life were able to face even a death of ultimate degradation and injustice. I've met Mexicans living in many degrees of pain and squalor, but I've known very few who face life or death without a belief that God is there and cares. In fact, if you confess to a typical Mexican that you doubt whether God exists or gives a damn, he will likely flash you the poor-pathetic-gringo-look and offer to buy you a beer.

Perhaps he has a point. While most Mexicans have little faith in the workings of democracy or the benefits of exercise, they pity the desperate fool who finds himself in a spiritual void. In our flight from moralism to unlimited freedom, have North Americans sold our souls to the …? Well, of course, we don't believe in him either.

In *Man's Search for Meaning*, Dr. Frankl contended that the depression, aggression, and addiction of Western society cannot be comprehended without recognizing the existential vacuum underlying them. He furthermore suggested that the Statue of Liberty should be supplemented by a Statue of Moral Responsibility, lest freedom degenerate into a meaningless existence.

Ironically, while Latinos do a majority of the physical suffering in the Americas, gringos do almost all of the clamoring for the right to assisted suicide. In Auschwitz, Frankl conducted doctor-assisted non-suicides, dissuading comrades from offing themselves by helping them find meaning in all life, even suffering. If Kevorkian were right, then Frankl was denying people dignity rather than restoring it. When would-be suicides argued that they had nothing more to expect from life, Frankl boldly suggested that "life was still expecting something from them."

I came to Mexico with the gringo values of effective-time-management and cleanliness-next-to-godliness; I came away with a deep conviction that life and death can be faced with purpose and courage. John Steinbeck once combined a Mexican folktale and a parable of Jesus to caution that the pearl of divine and family love should never be traded for the pearl of worldly wealth and leisure. Mexican Don Juan DeMarco (Johnny Dep) similarly enlightened his gringo psychologist (Marlon Brando) that all the questions in life worth asking have the same answer: love. For some reason, most of my brown friends don't have to be told this. They know people need reasons for living, not just resources.

Heading North on the highway from Zacatecas, I watched red ponies grazing in yellow daisies and ashen burros slumbering among brown corn-stalk pyramids. Slowly, the cactus took over—blue agave, grayish maguey, pale green organo, and red-fruited garambullo.

To the physical eye, the desert is a lifeless place. When seen under the midday sun, it appears still as a corpse and dry as a crypt. Yet, locals know the truth. As darkness closes in, the coyote and the tarantula come to life.

Like the biblical Samaritan woman, ancient Aztecs found living water in a parched land. Beneath a forbidding surface, the cactus gushes with moisture. For those who endure prickly discomfort, it provides the vegetable nopal, the tuna fruit, and the beverage tequila. As people draw near to death, they often sense more life in this equally forlorn prickly place than meets the eye.

When my mother lay dying from cancer and diabetes, a doctor proffered her a quicker exit to avoid the approaching days of pain. Instead, she hung on and suffered as humans often do, until her children and grandchildren arrived by car and plane. Though I'm not suggesting that Kevorkian's clients were taking the "coward's way out," neither can I endorse the politically correct notion that those who pass in agony fail to "die with dignity."

In a world where many suffer guilt from unresolved relations, my mother gave a precious gift in the midst of her pain. One day dialysis became impossible, which meant that afternoon's fifteen minutes of consciousness would be her last. I was choking and drowning on the knowledge that we were having our final conversation, but Mom simply squeezed my hand and spoke a concluding sentence: "I'll see you soon." I take her at her word.

Everything I know about facing death, I learned from my mother or those crazy Mexicans. Gracious mis amigos, hasta luego mi mama.

Made in the USA
Charleston, SC
03 August 2010